Anonymous

Light on current topics

Anonymous

Light on current topics

ISBN/EAN: 9783337270186

Printed in Europe, USA, Canada, Australia, Japan

Cover: Foto ©Andreas Hilbeck / pixelio.de

More available books at **www.hansebooks.com**

BENNETT LECTURES FOR 1895

BOSTON:
MASSACHUSETTS NEW-CHURCH UNION
1895

COPYRIGHT, 1895,
BY MASS. NEW-CHURCH UNION.

PREFACE.

The following chapters were originally in the form of lectures delivered in Boston early in the year 1895. With the exception of the first — which forms the Introduction and has been greatly abbreviated in order to avoid needless repetitions — they are here printed substantially as they were delivered. Pecuniary means for procuring and publishing them were afforded by a bequest of the late Mrs. Eleanor Bennett, an esteemed member of the Boston Society of the New Jerusalem, who left to the society a perpetual fund, the annual interest of which must be "devoted and expended for such books, publications, and for such other purposes as the trustees to be appointed by said society shall from time to time see fit to direct in the promulgation of the doctrines of the Swedenborgian, or New Church, so called."

It was thought by those having charge of this fund that no better use could be made of the income for the time being than to provide for a course of lectures, with the purpose of setting forth the teaching of the New Church on a few topics of living interest. In pursuance of this plan, certain subjects were selected, and writers invited to prepare papers upon them. No other object was considered, in the choice of topics, than the answering of questions on which light was really needed. In the choice of lecturers also, the only thought was to ensure honest and dispassionate treatment, without personal bias or prejudice. The one request made of each was that he would make a thorough study of his subject, and of the doctrines of the New Church in relation thereto. The lectures, as delivered, gave much satisfaction. It remains to be seen how far their influence will be extended by means of the printed volume.

J. R.

CONTENTS

	PAGE.
INTRODUCTION. *James Reed*.	1
THEOSOPHY AND RELIGION. *Frank Sewall*. . . .	13
THE RIGHT AND EXERCISE OF OWNERSHIP. *Julian K. Smyth*.	63
THE DIVINE LAW OF USE AND ITS APPLICATION TO INDUSTRIAL PROBLEMS. *Albert Mason*. .	94
THE RELATION OF THE CHURCH TO THE STATE AND TO SECULAR AFFAIRS. *Samuel S. Seward*.	118
PAUPERISM AND CRIME. *Theodore F. Wright*. . .	148
NATURAL AND SPIRITUAL HEALTH. *James Reed*. .	174

LIGHT ON CURRENT TOPICS

INTRODUCTION

JAMES REED

IT is a trite remark that we are living in a new age of the world, in which the lives and thoughts of men are undergoing a remarkable change. This statement is one which no man would think of denying. It is universally understood that during the nineteenth century, now nearing its close, a wonderful step forward has been taken in the march of human progress. The civilization of today is not that of a hundred years ago. Conditions which were then unknown, are now deemed indispensable to human happiness. To dwell upon the mechanical inventions and improvements of this age, would be the rehearsal of a threadbare subject; and yet it is a matter on which we never cease to congratulate ourselves. Perhaps we are a little proud of our railways and steamships, our telegraphs and telephones, our power-presses, looms, sewing-machines, and all the familiar appliances peculiar to our latter-day life; but whether we are proud or not (and a modest spirit would surely become us better than a boastful one), the fact remains indisputable that the results of the past century, as illustrated in the practical arts and sciences, are something marvellous. Nor does any one imagine that we have reached the end of them. The only question which we ask one of another is, "What can be coming next?"

But it is not merely in these outward, visible things that the peculiar character of the age in which we live is manifested. The change is as great in men's habits of thought, as it is in the circumstances of their earthly lives. The air is full of new ideas; ideas which were unknown to preceding generations. When in the closing period of the last century the American Republic was born, and when, a few years later, the terrible ordeal of the French Revolution sounded the death knell of Feudalism in Europe, the world began to breathe a different atmosphere, and to establish new standards of judgment. Thus it was that the political conditions were changed; but the new movement did not stop there. We have seen a gradual enlargement of human sympathy, a growing sense of the great truth that all men belong to a universal brotherhood. By the improved facilities for communication, the ends of the earth are brought nearer together; and whatever is of interest to one nation is speedily brought to the attention of all other nations. A hundred years ago, the people of this country would hardly have known the fact if a war had broken out between China and Japan; but now the whole civilized world watches eagerly for the details of the conflict, and feels that it bears no distant relation to itself, and is likely to affect, in no small degree, the future history of all mankind. Assemblages like the Parliament of Religions, lately held in Chicago, were not only impossible, but inconceivable, in the years gone by. If that notable gathering had no other significance, it would be full of meaning from the simple fact that men of all nations and creeds came together in love and harmony under the same roof, and gave free expression to the faith which was in them.

When we consider all these changes, mechanical, political, economical, and moral, is it possible to believe that the spiritual states of men will show no advancement? In other words, can we suppose that their religious ideas will remain forever unaltered? Is the Christianity of the past to be the Christianity of the future? When the Lord Jesus Christ was in the world did He speak the final message which shall serve for the guidance of men on earth, and enlighten their pathway to heaven? or may we believe that He gave promise of a further unfolding of His truth when He declared, "I have yet many things to say unto you, but ye cannot bear them now"? It is the belief of those who call themselves New-Churchmen, that now is the time when that implied promise is fulfilled, and when new truth is revealed by Him out of the Holy Scriptures; so that the heart and centre of the great movement which all men recognize, is to be a new, a purer, and a higher Christianity.

These assertions, also, few thoughtful persons would be disposed to deny. Manifestly, there is a new spirit abroad among the churches. The old dogmas of the last century are, to a considerable extent, practically repudiated. Men cease to dwell on the wrath of God, and prefer to think of His love. They give less emphasis to doctrinal distinctions, and make more account of a good life. They are ceasing to magnify the differences between the various divisions of the Christian Church, and dwell with greater satisfaction on the points of agreement. Each denomination goes on in its accustomed way, cherishing certain things which are precious to itself, but with less rigor and less of the spirit of condemnation for others; believing, at least in some measure, that the great Christian brotherhood is of far more consequence than any single portion of it.

This changed state of affairs was substantially predicted in a series of books which was given to the world more than a hundred years ago. Their author was Emanuel Swedenborg, than whom no writer of modern times has been more completely misunderstood and misinterpreted. He was almost alone in his work, having but few in his own day to sympathize with him. Most of the books referred to were published anonymously. He neither desired nor claimed credit to himself for the truth that was in them. They were sent out into the world to be judged on their own merits, and not on the ground of any personal authority possessed by the writer. To him it was made clear that the elements of a great change were beginning to work in the minds of men. The former things, he said, would pass away; a new age was commencing. New spiritual influences were putting forth their power. A fresh impulse had been given to human thought, which would thenceforth be guided in new directions. The prophecies of the New Testament were receiving their fulfilment. Slowly indeed, would they be fully verified; but their final accomplishment would be sure and irresistible. If one were to seek for a description of the present age and of the possibilities which loom up before us, he could nowhere find a more perfect one than is foreshadowed in the writings of this man, who has been so poorly understood and so grossly misrepresented.

It is impossible in any brief statement to convey an adequate idea of the character and extent of Swedenborg's teachings. Suffice it to say that they have a bearing on every subject of human thought, and shed their influence over every duty and relation of human life. They contain a philosophy which unites the profoundest wisdom concerning God, with the simplest every-day experiences of man; which unfolds the order and method of creation; which makes clear the purposes of the Creator, and His relations with those whom He has created; which declares the structure and nature of the human mind; which embraces heaven as well as earth, and links together the life here and the life hereafter. This philosophy is not hostile to religion, but furnishes the very basis on which it rests. It does not discard the Sacred Scriptures, but presents them as the source from which all wisdom is derived; showing them to be not merely a revelation which God made once upon a time, but the embodied form of Divine and Infinite Truth, having immeasurable depths of meaning, and intended to serve throughout all ages as the medium of our Heavenly Father's presence — His voice speaking to His children. This opening of the Scriptures, with the completer knowledge which it gives of their contents, is the central point in the Christian System propounded by Swedenborg. All the other teachings contained in his writings, are collateral and secondary to this. Nor should it be forgotten that the Author of the Scriptures, the Being whose Divine Spirit and influence are represented as flowing through them, is set before us as the one personal God, made manifest in a Divinely-human nature as our Lord Jesus Christ.

Many persons have been repelled from an examination of Swedenborg's writings, by the impression that they are visionary and speculative in their character. With all due respect to those who hold this opinion, let me say that the fact is exactly the reverse. Those who accept the doctrines of the New Church, are led to do so because they find them altogether reasonable and practical. A distinguished Boston lawyer was accustomed to say that he believed them because they are the embodiment of good sound common-sense in religion. They do not make drafts on our credulity ; they do not require us to accept on faith, things that are not clearly understood ; but they appeal at every step to our rational faculties, connecting themselves with undoubted facts of science and philosophy. It is true that they lift our thoughts above this world and make the spiritual world real and living to us ; but they do not present it as a subject to feed our love of the marvellous, or to gratify any feverish desire for entering too familiarly into its secrets. They rebuke, instead of favoring, the practice (supposing it to be possible) of holding direct and open intercourse with spirits. Instead of these things, they point out the fundamental laws of being, showing that all nature is instinct with spirit, and that the natural world receives its life from the spiritual world, even as the body of man receives life from his soul. They do indeed declare to us that the spiritual world is ever present; that we ourselves are interiorly dwelling within it;

and that death is but the cessation of our connection with this outer world, and an awakening to the consciousness of spiritual and eternal realities. But these are things, which, if true, must be most desirable to know, and which, in their effect upon man's life, can hardly fail to be intensely practical; removing, as they do, much of the mystery which has obscured his future, and enlarging his field of vision, so as to give new significance to his present duties. The case is the same with all the teachings of the New Church as viewed by those who receive them. By the higher glimpses which they give of what is heavenly and Divine, they impart to our earthly existence fresh impulses and aspirations, which make life all the more worth living.

A knowledge of the relation between the spiritual and natural worlds, is an important aid in opening our understanding of the Scriptures. Indeed, it throws light upon every page of the inspired volume. It helps us to see what inspiration is, by revealing to us the source whence it proceeds. It explains the manner in which every supernatural appearance recorded in the Bible has taken place. Patriarchs, prophets, and apostles were able to see angels and spirits through the opening of their spiritual eyes. The angels who announced to the shepherds on the plains of Bethlehem the glad tidings of the Saviour's birth, and those who declared to the women at the sepulchre, the still more glorious news of His Resurrection, did not come flying down from some distant home in the skies, but were here all the while. The only difference was that the eyes of the shepherds and of the women were opened to behold them. A similar experience might be granted to us at this very moment if there were equal occasion for it. Heaven is just as near to men at the present day as it was in Bible times. We cannot clearly understand the life of our Lord on earth, and the experiences through which He passed, without some knowledge of the spiritual world as being the theatre of much that happened. The devil who tempted Him, the demons whom He cast out, and the angels who ministered unto Him, were all inhabitants of that world. By its constant presence with ourselves, the precious promises are fulfilled: "He shall give His angels charge over thee, to keep thee in all thy ways." "The angel of the Lord encampeth round about them that fear Him, and delivereth them." These and other sayings with which the Word of God abounds, become intelligible when we recognize the existence of a real inner world which is always present to those who dwell on earth, imparting to them in thousands of unseen ways its varied influences.

It is not the purpose of these lectures to enlarge upon, or even to define, any particular doctrines of the New Church. They will, however, aim to impress the fact that those doctrines constitute a system of spiritual laws, by which all the conditions and relations of human life are illuminated. One fact regarding them deserves special mention. While, as has been intimated, they present to the thoughts much that is new, while they penetrate more deeply to the heart and origin of things, they are not destructive in their character; they do no violence to anything which past ages have rightly cherished and revered. By the opening of the Scriptures, and by the enlargement of the field of spiritual knowledge, new light is indeed thrown upon all subjects, but with full recognition of the fact that the Lord has been present with His people, and has dealt with them according to their need, as lovingly in the generations that are past as He does now, or as He will continue to do in the time to come. The truth is, man is growing. He cannot always remain in the same stage of his development. He cannot always be governed by the same standards. But as he ascends on the successive steps of his progress, he should know and feel that the privileges which he enjoys would have been impossible unless the way for them had been prepared by the experiences of his fathers; and that all which his fathers have gained, freed from its defects and errors, is his to cherish and to hold, as the foundation of what is new and distinctive in his own special phase of human advancement.

It would be strange if the intense mental activity of this new age did not give rise to many ideas and theories of a questionable character. Together with grand and true teachings would naturally appear such as are evil and erroneous. What our Lord says about the danger of "false Christs and false prophets" surely has its application here. Amid the claimants to our favor, so numerous, so varied, and so conflicting, it is quite impossible that all should be worthy of acceptance. In these latter days theosophy raises its head under new guises; communism and socialism demand fresh consideration; the air is full of speculations regarding the causes of poverty and the modes of relieving or abolishing it; the relations between church and state, employers and employed, capital and labor, are unceasingly agitated; tremendous claims are made on behalf of subtle and (so-called) spiritual influences as affecting bodily health. Every man is invited, yea, almost compelled, to form an opinion on one or all of these and other matters respecting which so many theories are advanced in the name of the New Age. To the New-Church believer it is of interest to know what light is thrown upon them by the doctrines he professes. He is indeed prepared to find, as was previously intimated, that those doctrines illuminate all subjects, and furnish the needful means of distinguishing between the true and the false prophets. If this supposition is to any extent correct, the discussion pursued in the following lectures will have interest, not merely for special students, but for general readers likewise.

Let us, then, emphasize the fact that the problems

of the age in which we live are such as can be dealt with only by a new revelation of truth from on high, a deeper unfolding of the genuine spirit and meaning of Christianity, a fresh bringing-forth of the treasures which lie hidden in the Word of God. Surely, if the former things are to pass away, and all things are really to be made new, there cannot fail to be, as the central and vitalizing influence, a better knowledge of God, and a nearer and clearer relationship with Him, than previous ages have known. The New Jerusalem, as seen by the apostle John, was not in heaven, but was coming down from God out of heaven. It therefore describes, with its beautiful imagery, what will exist in the future time upon this earth. Chief among the promises, as showing the source whence all other blessings will flow, is this: "Behold, the tabernacle of God is with men, and He will dwell with them and they shall be His people, and God Himself shall be with them, their God."

THEOSOPHY AND RELIGION

FRANK SEWALL

Canst thou by searching find out God? — JOB xi. 7.

As universal as religion * is the desire of man to "find out God." The nature of religion itself may be defined as the desire of man to place himself in relation with a being higher than himself. The knowledge sought for as the basis of such a relation, assumes in the history of man three forms which may be designated as:

I. Revelation and Doctrine thence derived, or Theology in the commonly accepted sense.

II. Philosophy,† or the process of rational thinking.

---

* "If it were possible that a human being could be without religion it would be impossible to give him religion." (Froebel. Education of Man.)

"The assertion that religion is entirely lacking in any tribe is based on a misconception of the definition of religion. Practices implying a belief in supernatural powers which may be propitiated, are found in every tribe." (History of the Mental Growth of Mankind. John S. Hittell. Henry Holt & Co: 1893.)

† With the Greeks Philosophy embraced Theology as its highest

13

III. Theosophy or knowledge by immediate vision.* To learn the comparative value of these methods, and how they enter into the religious life of mankind at the present day, is the object of the present inquiry. The second or philosophic method enters practically into all methods of discovery, and while it may be held theoretically by some as capable of arriving by itself at a true knowledge of good, yet as a matter of fact the revealed knowledge of God has existed before any known system of philosophy.

---

domain. Aristotle defines it as the perception of ends, the knowledge of the " First Cause," of " the First Mover," and of " the Good." (Metaph. vi.; xii.)

Plato represents Theology as the representation of the Divine qualities to man in order that man may grow up to Divine ideals. (Republic, 379.)

But these are all quite distinct from the Theology based upon objective revelation or the "knowing" of the Gospel as defined by St. John in the words: " This is life eternal: that they may know Thee, the only true God, and Jesus Christ whom Thou hast sent." (ST. JOHN xvii. 3.)

*" Theosophy, as its derivation implies, is a term used to denote those forms of philosophic and religious thought which claim a special insight into the Divine nature. . . . The theosophist is most at his ease when moving in the circle of the Divine essence into which he seems to claim absolute insight."

" Swedenborg is usually reckoned among the theosophists, and some parts of his theory justify this conclusion; but his system as a whole has little in common with those speculative constructions of the Divine nature which form the essence of theosophy, as strictly understood." (Professor Andrew Seth, Art. Theosophy in Encycl. Brittanica, 1888.)

Our discussion will mainly treat therefore of the relation of Theosophy to Revealed Religion.

It is customary with those who treat the history of religion according to what is styled the scientific method, as affording an example of purely natural evolution, to begin with what is called the Animistic stage. By Animism is meant a perception of some power in natural objects, in the elements, and also in idols, fetiches, and charms, which is identified with personality, which causes dread and fear, which operates supernaturally, and which is appeased by human worship, especially by sacrifices. This, it is said by the evolutionists, is the first beginning of religion and religious worship.*

The inference that it is so is drawn from the fact that such is the religion of many existing tribes still in the lowest stages of barbarism, or, according to the theory, nearest the brute stage from which they have emerged. The fear of the dead was, according to these writers, the first sense of the supernatural, and the effort to keep them quiet in their graves was the first motive of worship.

But in drawing this inference as to the origin of religion the fact is overlooked that the animism or nature worship of these so-called "primitive men" is not essentially different from that of the most advanced and civilized races of mankind at the time

---

* See Herbert Spencer's various treatises on the origin of the religious sentiment.

when written history commences. Indeed it still exists in the Shintoism of Japan — the most advanced of the non-Christian nations. The truly scientific method then, requires that instead of inventing a prehistoric origin to suit our theory, we shall ask what these races, both civilized and barbarous, who are now or who within the historic period have been in the practice of animistic worship, have to say as to the origin of religion with them.

Diodorus Siculus (I. 94), the historian of the time of Augustus, writes that:

"The Egyptians believed that their laws came from Hermos; Cretans that Minos, their law-giver, obtained his laws from Zeus. The Lacedæmonians believed that Lycurgus obtained his from Apollo; the Aryans that Zathraustus (Zoroaster) obtained his from the Good Spirit. According to the Getæ, Zamolxis claimed that his were from Hestia, and Moses claimed to have derived his from Jao."

Both Max Müller and the Duke of Argyle agree in the statement, that "wherever we can trace back a religion to its first beginnings, we find it free from many blemishes that affected it in later stages."

The ancient region of Akkad — the Mesopotamian Valley — was, with Egypt, the scene of the most degraded forms of Animism, that is of nature and idol worship.* It was out of this land and this animistic worship that Abram was called two thousand years

---

* "The religion of Akkad was largely that of nature worship;

before Christ. And today in the British Museum may be seen a tablet on which is written perhaps the oldest religious inscription in the world, taken from a temple of the patron deity of the city of Ur, upon which Abram himself may have looked. It shows what lofty and pure traditions still survived in the midst of all the degraded nature-worship of his time. The following are some lines from this inscription:

> Lord, Prince of Gods of heaven and earth, whose mandate is exalted.
> Father, God enlightening earth.
> Lord, Good God, of Gods the Prince.
> Father mine, of life the Giver, cherishing, beholding, all!
> Thou thy will in heaven revealest; Thee celestial spirits praise!*

Renouf, in his Hibbert Lectures (p. 103), quotes an ancient Egyptian Hymn:

> God is one and alone and there is no other with Him;

---

when the Semites entered the land, nature worship had developed into Polytheism; the sorcerer had become priest.

"But in the higher and more gifted minds of ancient Akkad we find a pure monotheism.

"In Egypt there were few traces of animal worship in the first dynasties: it is rarely, if ever, referred to between the ages of Khufu (the builder of the Great Pyramid) and Rameses. After the days of Rameses the worship grew and developed, and serves to show the degradation of the national religion." (Davis. Introd. to Book of the Dead, p. 35.)

* Quoted in the introduction to the "Book of the Dead." Translated from Pierret, by Davis, 1894.

God is a Spirit, a hidden Spirit, the Divine Spirit.
God is eternal.
God is the Truth: He lives by Truth: He is the king of Truth.
God is Life and man lives through Him.

(Cited by Davis.)

The following is a hymn to Râ in the Egyptian "Book of the Dead:"*

Hail, thou who art come as Time, who hast been creator of all the gods!
Hail, supreme among the gods:
Hail, thou hast slain the guilty; thou hast destroyed Apap (the Serpent of Darkness).

I am Tum, a Being who is One above.
I am Râ in His first supremacy,
I am the great God; the self-existing; I was yesterday, I know the tomorrow.

I am Tum, the only Being in Nu:
I am the Sun when he rises:
I am the Great God creating Himself:
I am the Morning: I know the Gate.

(Davis's Translation.)

---

* The "Book of the Dead" was first translated and published in 1842, by Lepsius, from a collection of papyri. It contains 165 chapters, and "holds the first and principal place" says Tiele, "among the sources of our knowledge of the ancient Egyptian religion. It was believed to be inspired by Thoth himself. Thoth himself speaks in it. It was written by his finger. Its prayers were learned by heart and had been handed down from time immemorial. It depicts a worship that prevailed over five thousand years ago.

Taking our stand then in this animistic stage of the history of religion,* and reaching backward toward the origin of religion we find that far from tracing its rise from a lower stage of religious feeling, it points to its source in a higher; far from deriving its religious sentiment as a natural growth from animal instincts, it points to a great primitive source in a Divine revelation; far from building its idea of God out of innumerable ghosts of the dead, it points to One supreme Deity, who is good, the ruler of all, the creator of all. Finally, far from starting with elementary forces, or with the natural elements, as objects

---

* " We find in Egypt the deified attributes of one God, together with the worship of animals and of the heavenly bodies." (Davis. Introd. to Book of the Dead.)

" In the light of modern research modern investigators do not find it difficult to go behind the wild, gaudy, coarse, and often ridiculous polytheism, which was the religion of the multitude, to the subtle and often sublime monotheism which was the heart and conscience of the educated classes.

" Over six thousand years ago the Egyptians came from Arabia to Africa and found a race unlike themselves, and imposed a Semitic dialect upon the anterior people of the lower Nile.

" While we find the lower races grovelling in the most degraded form of fetich worship, we find the higher holding a creed almost identical with the monotheism of Moses and of Job." (Davis. Introd. to Book of the Dead, p. 40.)

" To the general public their (the Egyptians') religion was a polytheism of a multitudinous and gross character. To the intelligent, the learned, the initiated, it was a system combining strict monotheism with a metaphysical speculative philosophy on the two great subjects, the nature of God and the destiny of man." (Lenormant. *Les Premières Civilizations.*)

of worship, and gradually coming to the idea of a Divine personality,* we find the feeling of Divine personality to be at the very root and spring of religion always and everywhere; and that the universal magic by which to turn anything, whether light, or sky, or sun, or man, or image, or stream, or bit of stone, or clay, into an object of worship was to personify it — to make it a person and so to liken it to God.

Thus Animism in the light not of theory but of actual tradition and experience in places and in times when Animism prevailed, reveals these four secrets regarding the religion that was before:

I. That at some time God has revealed Himself and communicated a knowledge of the Divine to men. †

---

* " How," says Max Müller, " do these savages when they pick up a stone, pick up at the same time the concept of a supernatural power, of 'spirit,' of 'a God'? Fetichism is not a primary form of religion, nor is the fetich the object worshipped." (Müller. Origin of Religion.)

Gladstone maintains that the mythical system of the Greeks, and the theology of the Iliad and Odyssey, are the corrupted form of Divine Revelation imparted to man in his infancy. (See Homeric Studies.)

† In the first chapter of the "Book of the Dead" we read: "It has been enjoined by Râ to Thoth to make Truth the Word of Osiris against his foes." In the sixty-fourth chapter: "It is written by the finger of Thoth — a manifestation of Truth and Goodness. There is no book like it. Man hath not spoken it, neither hath ear heard it."

II. That God is One.*

III. That the One God, the revealer of all, and the origin of all is a Person.†

IV. That the earliest religion was of a pure and elevated type and that in its descent it assumed the forms of a symbolism more and more gross and external.

The historical inquiry into the origin of religion enables us to appreciate more fully Swedenborg's

---

* " Had the Egyptians any idea of one God?—in other words is their religion a complex structure raised upon a recognized monotheistic foundation? The Egyptian religious writers are held by M. de Rougé to give an affirmative answer to this question. They speak of one supreme being, self-existent, self-producing, the creator of heaven and earth, called the double god or double being, as the parent of a second manifestation. From the idea of a supreme deity, at once father and mother, producing a second form, probably originated a first triad, like the triads of father, mother, and son, frequent in the Egyptian mythology." (Encycl. Brittanica, Art. Egypt. Reginald Stuart Poole.)

" The gods of the Pantheon were manifestations of the One Being in his various capacities.

" Even in the grossest period of the Egyptian religion the doctrine of one God was taught.

" The 'Nutar Nutra' of Egypt exactly corresponds to the Hebrew El Shaddai." (Pierret, in Introd. to Book of the Dead.)

† " The Aryan, the Semitic, the Turanian race, all had a primitive religion," says Max Müller. " The highest god, that is the Supreme, received the same name in India, in Greece, in Italy, in Germany. Thousands of years before Homer and the Vedas, the ancestors of our Indo-European race worshipped an unseen Being under the same name — the best, the highest, Light and Sky, Dyous Piter, Heaven, Father, Our Father in Heaven."

teaching regarding the Ancient Word existing before our Bible, from which, he asserts, were taken the early chapters of Genesis, or those great world-poems of a Golden Age, a Flood, and an Ark — traces of which are found in the sacred books of all the great historic religions.* This Eden stage of mankind was one of childlike innocence in which man enjoyed an immediate knowledge of God and open intercourse

---

* "To us it seems that so far as the men of history speak at all, it is in favor of a primitive race of men, not indeed equipped with all the arts and appliances of our modern civilization, but substantially civilized, possessing language, thought, intelligence; conscious of a Divine Being; quick to form the conception of tools, and to frame them as it needed them; early developing many of the useful and elegant arts, and only sinking by degrees and under peculiar circumstances into the savage condition.

"It will scarcely be denied that the mythical traditions of almost all nations place at the beginning of human history a time of happiness and perfection, a 'golden age' which has no features of savagery or barbarism, but many of civilization and refinement.

"In the Zendevesta Jemshid, Yima-Khahaeta, the first Aryan king, removes, with his subjects, to a secluded spot where both he and they enjoy uninterrupted happiness. In this place 'was neither overbearing nor mean-spiritedness, neither stupidity nor violence, neither poverty nor deceit, neither puniness nor deformity, neither huge teeth, nor bodies beyond the usual measure.'" (Vendidad. Fargard, II. 29.)

"The Chinese spoke of a 'first heaven,' an age of innocence when 'the whole creation enjoyed a state of happiness; when every thing was beautiful, every thing was good; all beings were perfect in their kind.'" (Faber. Horae Mosaicae, p. 147.)

"Mexican tradition tells of the 'Golden age of Tezeuco.'" (Prescott. Conquest of Mexico, chapter vi.)

"Peruvian history commences with two 'Children of the Sun'

with heaven. This was not acquired through reason, but was the result of man's being an uncorrupted creature, existing in the perfect order of creation and in perfect harmony with his environment, and so attuned to the harmony of the universe that every experience struck a true note and told him the truth of all. To this uncorrupted Adam all nature was transparent with its meaning, and that meaning was heaven and God.* The Fall of man consisted in the

---

who established a civilized community on the borders of Lake Titicaca." (Prescott. Conquest of Peru, chap. i., p. 8.)

"The Greek Hesiod in his Works and Days (II. 109), describes how 'The immortal gods that tread the courts of heaven first made a golden race of mortal men,'" etc.

"Egypt and Babylonia have monuments to show which antedate probably all others upon the earth's surface."

"In Egypt it is notorious that there is no indication of any early period of savagery or barbarism."

"In Babylonia there is more indication of early rudeness, . . . but on the other hand there are not wanting signs of an advanced state of certain arts, even in its very earliest times." (Introduction to The Origin of Nations, George Rawlinson, M. A., 1881.)

* " I will draw a picture of the two states of man : first of his state of integrity, which was most perfect; and then of that perverted and imperfect state in which as degenerated mortals we live this day. . . .

"To begin then with man in his state of integrity and complete perfection. In such a man we may conceive to have existed such a complete continuity throughout the parts of the system that every motion proceeding with a free course from his grosser parts or principles could arrive through an uninterrupted connection at his most subtle substance or active principle, there being nothing in the way which could cause the least obstruction. Such a man may be com-

entrance of self-love and the consequent pride of intelligence which put man out of this perfect harmony and wisdom, and closed this immediate vision. Thenceforward man could not read the truth and know God from the instinct of the will, but must learn of Him through the outward way of the intellect.

---

pared to the world itself, in which all things are contiguous from the sun to the bottom of the atmosphere; thus the solar rays proceed with an uninterrupted course, and almost instantaneously, by means of the contiguity of the more subtle or grosser elements through which they pass, through the ether into the air, till they arrive at the eye and operate upon it, by virtue of such connection, as if they were present; for contiguity occasions the appearance of presence. . . .

"The man thus formed in whom all the parts conspired to receive the motions of all the elements and to carry them successively, when received, through a contiguous medium, to the most subtle active principle, must be deemed the most perfect and the first of all men, being one in whom the connection of ends and means is continuous and unbroken. Such a most perfect material and acting being would, in a short time, acquire by the aid of the senses alone, all the philosophy and experimental science natural to him.

"But when every modification in the world, of whatever nature, had thus arrived at its ultimate or at his soul, it necessarily follows that his knowledge and attainments would then stop, and that he would regard and venerate, with a most profound admiration, those other and infinite things that exceeded the bounds of his intelligence; that is, that most vast Infinite — infinitely intelligent, infinitely provident — which begins where man and his finite faculties, intelligence, and providence, terminate; he would see that in this Infinite all things have their being, and that from it all things have their existence." (Swedenborg. Principia, Part I., chap. I.)

The age of symbols followed, when the ancient truths were preserved in symbolic forms, and when all symbolic worship was instituted. At first the symbol was transparent, and full of spiritual light; but gradually it became clouded and opaque, until at last all the inner meaning was lost and only the shadow remained. This was the stage of the animism, or nature worship, above described. Then followed the "nomistic" stage of religion, when a Divine religion and its monotheistic worship could only be preserved by the written "Law and the Prophets," to preserve which the Jewish or Semitic race was providentially raised up.

When at length this law was becoming of "no effect through their traditions," then in Jesus Christ the Word was made flesh. But he came not to destroy the written tradition, but to fulfil it; to show rather that He was Himself the essential Word or Wisdom which lay concealed in the Old Testament; that what He did was "in order that the Scriptures might be fulfilled," and so "beginning with Moses and all the prophets, He expounded unto His disciples, in all the Scriptures, the things concerning Himself."

The wisdom lost to man since Eden was therefore restored, but restored only in Him in Whom the Word was fulfilled. He also gave to men the New Testament containing the record of His life and teachings, written by those to whom He had promised that His spirit should bring to remembrance all the things He had said unto them.

Such then is the tradition of Divine knowledge which is possessed by Christians in their Sacred Scriptures.*

No one who studies the history of religions can fail to see, however, that from that earliest revelation or knowledge of God to which all the great historic religions point back, there have been other channels of tradition more or less imperfect besides that of the Hebraic Scriptures. These other channels, while it is not claimed for them that they were shaped by Divine dictation, as in the case of the Semitic Word, and while they exhibit the freer play of human imagination and genius, were nevertheless instrumental in preserving among other races the early knowledge of God.

Our own race which is not Semitic but Aryan, was constituted for a different office in connection with Divine revelation than that of the Hebrews, and it was through these other channels that our ancient forefathers in Asia received these earliest traditions of the Golden Age and the worship of the "Heaven Father."

At the beginning of his translations of the Vedic Hymns, F. Max Müller places the hymn "To the Unknown God," and in his preface he gives his

---

* See Swedenborg. "Doctrine of the Sacred Scripture."

reason for doing so in a passage which I have quoted in the note below.*

---

* "I have often been asked why I began my translation of the Rig-Veda with the hymns addressed to the Maruts or the Storm-gods.

"There are few hymns which place the original character of the so-called deities to whom they are addressed in so clear a light as the hymns addressed to the Maruts or Storm-gods. Storms which root up the trees of the forest, lightning, thunder, and showers of rain, are the background from which the Maruts in their personal and dramatic character rise before our eyes. . . . After a time the Storm-gods in India, like the Storm-gods in other countries, obtain a kind of supremacy and are invoked by themselves as if there were no other gods beside them. In most of the later native dictionaries . . . Marut is given as a synonym of deva, or god in general. . . . The hymns addressed to the Maruts enable us to watch the successive stages in the development of so-called deities more clearly than in any other hymns. Whatever Zeus became afterwards, he was originally conceived as Dyaus, the bright sky. . . . With regard to Mar-ut, I have myself no doubt whatever that Mar-ut comes from the root M AR in the sense of grinding, crushing, pounding. . . . Professor Kuhn's idea that the name of the Maruts was derived from the root M AR, to die, and that the Maruts were originally conceived as the souls of the departed, and afterwards as *ghosts, spirits, winds,* and lastly as storms, derives no support from the Veda.

"In order to show, however, that the Vedic hymns, though they begin with a description of the most striking phenomena of nature, are by no means confined to that narrow sphere, but *rise in the end to the most sublime conception of a supreme Deity*, I have placed one hymn, that addressed to the Unknown God, at the head of my collection. This will clear me, I hope, of the very unfair suspicion that by beginning my translation of the Rig-Veda with hymns celebrating the wild forces of nature only, I had wished to represent the Vedic religion as nature-worship and nothing else." (F. Max Müller. Introduction to the Vedic Hymns, Part I. pp. xxiv.–xxvii. Sacred Books of the East. Oxford, at the Clarendon Press.)

The hymn is as follows:

TO THE UNKNOWN GOD.*

1. In the beginning there arose the Golden Child: as soon as born he alone was lord of all that is. He established the earth and this heaven:—Who is the God to whom we shall offer sacrifice?

2. He who gives breath, he who gives strength, whose command all the bright gods revere, whose shadow is immortality, whose shadow is death:—Who is the God to whom we shall offer sacrifice?

3. He who through his might became the sole being of the breathing and twinkling world, who governs all this, man and beast:—Who is the God to whom we shall offer sacrifice?

4. He through whom the awful heaven and the earth were made fast, he through whom the ether was established, and the firmament; he who measured the air in the sky:—Who is the God to whom we shall offer sacrifice?

5. He to whom heaven and earth, standing forever by his will, look up, trembling in their mind: he over whom the risen sun shines forth:—Who is he to whom we shall offer sacrifice?

6. When the great waters went everywhere, holding the germ and generating light, then there arose from them the breath of the gods:—Who is the God to whom we shall offer sacrifice?

7. He who by his might looked even over the waters which held power, and generated the sacrifice, he who alone is God above all gods:—Who is the God to whom we shall offer sacrifice?

8. May he not hurt us, he who is the begotten of the earth,

---

* Ka, Who?

or he, the righteous, who begat the heaven; he who also begat the bright and mighty waters:—Who is the God to whom we shall offer sacrifice?

9. Pragapati, no other than thou embraces all these created things. May that be ours which we desire when sacrificing to thee: may we become lords of wealth!*

Though, it may be, the same Ancient Word of the age of the transparent symbol, the primitive revelation was handed down, not in the form of unalterable law and ritual, and by a theocracy and priesthood, institutions compatible with the external, sensuous mind of the Semitic race, but in the form of the great mythical powers of the Hindus, the Vedas † and the

---

* F. Max Müller admits that "the conception of one God which pervades the whole of this hymn" affords a reason for suspecting it as modern to those who think that the conception of one God followed the conception of many gods as recognized in the various aspects of nature, such as the gods of the sky, the sun, the storms, or the fire. Nevertheless, he contends that the hymn cannot be so modern, but that it existed before 1000 B. C., *before* the Brahmana and the Mantra period.

† "It (the Veda) is, by the Indians themselves divided into two grand portions — *mantra* and *brahmana* (which words we may render, though not literally, by 'worship' and 'theology'); and this division, as is not always the case with one of native origin, is in fact an essential one, separating two widely different classes of writings, which stand related to one another as canonized art on the one hand and canonized explication, dogmatical, exegetical, historical, prescriptive, on the other; which in the main are widely removed in time and represent two distinct periods of religious development, and of which one is in verse and the other in prose. The latter, the *brahmana*, is made up of various single works, which also bear the

Avesta, and, later, of the Homeric poems of the Greeks.

The Aryan mind, unlike the Semitic, is distinctly intellectual. It is given to looking behind the symbol to the reality within and to breaking away from the bondage of fixed traditions and enjoying the freedom of reason and of action. This free spirit, the real "light of Asia," came down into the plains of Akkad where lay the remains of Animism, as we

---

name of *brahmana*, and other kindred writings such as the Aranyakas and Upanishads. The first portion, *mantra*, consists of the four works commonly known as Rig-Veda, Sâma-Veda, Yajur-Veda, Atharva-Veda — the Vedas in contradistinction to the Veda.

"The general form of the Vedas is tnat of lyrical poetry. They contain the songs in which the first ancestors of the Hindu people, at the very dawn of their existence as a separate nation, while they were still only on the threshold of the great country they were afterwards to fill with their civilization, praised the gods, extolled heroic deeds, and sang of other matters which kindled their poetic fervor. As in point of time they are probably the most ancient existing literary records of our race, so, at any rate, in the progression of literary development they are, beyond dispute, the earliest we possess, the most complete representation which has been preserved to modern times of that primitive lyrical epoch which theory assumes as the earliest in the literary history of any people. . . . No great people, surely, ever presented the spectacle of a development more predominantly religious; none ever grounded its whole fabric of social and political life more on a religious basis; none ever meditated more deeply and exclusively on things supernatural; none ever rose, on the one hand, higher into the airy regions of a purely speculative creed, or sank, on the other, deeper into degrading superstitions — the two extremes to which such a tendency naturally leads." (William Dwight Whitney. The Vedas, in "Oriental and Linguistic Studies." New York: 1873.)

see it in the impressive monuments of Babylon and Assyria.* But here the stream of tradition divided. On the one hand toward the west arose with the mighty Persian nation the beautiful religion of the Parsees, founded on the teachings of Zoroaster, in which we can easily discern that star in the east which led the wise men to worship, when the time should

---

* "As the Parsis are the ruins of a people, so are their sacred books the ruins of a religion. There has been no other great belief in the world that has left such poor and meagre monuments of its past splendor. . . . By the help of the Parsi religion and the Avesta we are enabled to go back to the very heart of that most momentous period in the history of religious thought, which saw the blending of the Aryan mind and the Semitic, and thus opened the second stage of Aryan thought." (Darmesteter. Introduction to the Zend-Avesta, p. xi.)

"The key to the Avesta is not the Pahlavi, but the Veda. The Avesta and the Veda are two echoes of the same voice, the influx of one and the same thought; the Vedas, therefore, are both the best lexicon and the best commentary on the Avesta.

"The traditional school replied that relationship is not identity . . . that the Vedic language and the Vedas are quite unable to teach us what became in Persia of those elements which are common to the two systems, a thing which tradition alone can teach us.

"It cannot happen that the tradition and the Veda will really contradict one another, if we care to ask from each only what it knows. The first place belongs to tradition as it comes straight from the Avesta. The Veda is not the past of the Avesta, as the Avesta is the past of tradition; the Avesta and Veda are not derived from one another, but from one and the same original, diversely altered in each." (p. xxviii.)

"What was the religion of the Magi which we find reflected in the Avesta, and whence did it arise? . . .

"We have tried in another book (Ormazd and Ahriman, Paris,

come, at the manger in Bethlehem. The same receptivity toward a Divine religion revealed from above, but seeking an incarnation in a Divine Humanity, is exhibited by the Greek branch of the Aryan family. The Hellenic intellect and love of the beautiful as the ultimation of the Divine in the outward forms, both of literature and of art, made this people peculiarly fitted to be the receptacle of the sacred revelation handed down unmarred but

---

1877), to show that the religion of the Magi is derived from the same source as that of the Indian Rishis, that is from the religion followed by the common forefathers of the Iramian and the Indians, the Indo-Iramian religion. . . . There were in the Indo-Iramian religion a latent monotheism and an unconscious dualism, both of which in the further development of Indian thought slowly disappeared. . . . The God that has established the laws in nature is the Heaven God. He is the greatest of gods since there is nothing above him nor outside of him; he has made everything since everything is produced or takes place in him; he is the wisest of all gods, since with his eyes, the sun, moon, and stars, he sees everything." (See the Supreme God in the Indo-European Mythology, in the *Contemporary Review*, October, 1879, p. 283.)

"This god was named either after his bodily nature, Varana, 'the all-embracing sky,' (*Οὐρανός*, or Dyaus, 'the shining sky') or after his spiritual attributes, Asura, 'the Lord,' Asura Visvavedas, 'the all-knowing Lord,' Asura Mazahâ, 'the Lord of high knowledge,' or perhaps 'the Lord who bestows intelligence.'" (p. lvii.)

"In the middle of the Vedic period, Indra, the dazzling god of storm, rose to supremacy in the Indian Pantheon, and outshone Varuna, with the roar and splendor of his feats, but soon to give way to a new and mystic king, Prayer or Brahman." Cf. The Supreme God, p. 287. (Darmesteter. Introduction to the Zend-Avesta, p. lix.)

unopened in the casket of Jewish Scripture.* The Greeks furnished the intellect, in whose understanding of the revealed truth a new will of good might be formed, and a new path opened to a knowledge of the Divine, but always the path of truth revealed in the Word, or in that revelation by which God, as the Truth, has made Himself forever objective to man, and so forever to be studied from without and from above.†

But while the intellect of the race was being prepared in the West by the splendid discipline of the Greek philosophy for the ultimate reception of this Word from heaven Who should come as the One sent of God and born of God, there was another tendency growing up in the East, which originating in the same source — the ancient Vedic hymns of India

---

* "Greece supplied the intellectual factor under the new dispensation of Christianity, as truly as the Hebrew race supplied us with the spiritual force which was to regenerate the heart and will of man. And this was done for millions who knew but little but the name either of Greeks or Jews." (The Hon. Wm. E. Gladstone, in Article, Greece and Christianity. *Nineteenth Century*, October, 1891.)

† "Except ye believe in this Christ ye shall die in your sins." For the sin into which man's selfish nature continually leads him, can never be overcome except in obedience to a truth which is not of the will which sins, but which comes from above, and can command that will with an authority above its own — the authority of God. The corrupted will cannot lift a man up by any vision of its own. "No man hath ascended up to heaven but he that first came down from heaven, even the Son of Man which is in heaven." A saving religion could never be developed from man but must come from above.

— brought into play other mental traits of the race and have led to such modifications of the sacred traditions as to convert them into the very antipodes of the Christian religion.* This is the religion of Buddha, and forms the substance of what is known popularly as Occultism and Orientalism, and with some adaptation to forms of thought and life, appears in the theosophy of the present time.

In the "Working Glossary for Theosophic Students," we find this definition: "Theosophy, Divine wisdom; the wisdom of the gods obtained through the gods, not however by revelation, but through individual aspiration and experience."

Theosophy would seem to mean, according to its accepted expounders, Wisdom-religion, or the religion which consists in man's possessing Divine wisdom. But "Divine wisdom" means here not the wisdom of One God imparted to men, but the wisdom of the gods, that is, of each man in becoming a god to himself. For, according to theosophy, there is no one supreme God of whom wisdom is an attribute, be-

---

*One of the most striking characteristics of the Hindu race has been its longing after something vague, shadowy, indistinct, existing not on the plane of matter; and the mind is therefore trained to look inward for that which shall make us happy. It is this tendency that has given rise to the innumerable schools of occultism. ... You, on the other hand, have developed a stupendous momentum on the plane of matter; an immense Kinetic energy on the plane of intellect. (Chakravati's Address. Theosophical Congress: Chicago. 1893.)

cause there is no one personal God,* but there is a wisdom called Divine and all who attain to it are gods. Theosophy means, therefore, at once a knowledge of God and a knowledge of no God, for the knowledge of God when attained is either the knowledge in each man of himself as God and of God as many and not One ; or else it means our being lost in that abyss of no-knowledge which is prior to all personality and all godhood, and which is called the absolute and formless all.†

In its theology and cosmogony, theosophy may be regarded as of Brahminic origin, while its ethics or practical precepts are Buddhistic. Gautama, Buddha, or the "wise one" obtained his wisdom, the *Budhi*, from the Brahm of the Vedic hymns and teachers. The Brahm or Supreme Spirit, originally in the Ancient Aryan conception a Personal Deity — the "Heaven Father" — has become in the course of Vedic tradition the reason or wisdom itself in the abstract, then the Written Scripture containing the hidden wisdom within, and at length personified

---

* See " A Key to Theosophy," by H. P. Blavatsky.

† " The Atma or Spirit, is something which cannot be understood either by words, or by hearing, or by intellect. They alone who resort to the spirit have the light of the spirit brought to their own spirit." (A "sloka" from the Upanishads, read by Prof. G. N. Chakravati of Allahabad, India. Theosophic Congress: Chicago. 1893.)

again as the all-ruling Deity.* Against the system of caste and exclusion which the teaching of this occult wisdom of the Brahm and the performance of its symbolic rites had developed, Buddha came as the great protestant claiming the right to "private interpretation" of the Aryan Bible, and declaring for the abolishment of external priesthood and worship. The path to the hidden wisdom was to be found in self-knowledge and in self-conquest alone. External tradition and authority were of avail no more. In this extreme and fatal reaction we find that impulse which led to the rejection of all historic and objective standards of Divine truth — the substitution of immediate intuitive knowledge for supernatural revelation.†

It is not unlike that movement of the Sophists in Greece, nearly contemporary with the rise of Buddhism, which, carried away with the idea of the supe-

---

*See " Outlines of the History of the Ancient Religions." G. P. Tiele. p. 125.

† " True theosophy is the eternal undying truth which cannot be brought down to the plane of speech or intellect. It can be taught on the plane of intellect, but once on the plane of intellect it ceases to be spirit. In its highest essence theosophy is ineffable.

" The attempt of modern theosophy is to bring home to the minds of men once more, that behind the more or less translucent roots of every religion shines the glorious sun of Truth, and that spiritual knowledge as spiritual inspiration is not the birthright of any particular part of the earth. It says to every man, In your own religion if you dig deep enough you will find the truth." (Chakravati. Chicago Address. 1893.)

riority of mind and of "man as the measure of all things," finally proclaimed every man to be the sole source of truth to himself. And very much as Socrates was ranked among the Sophists, while really he was the first to overthrow their error by his principle of the one absolute Truth and Good over against all these individual conceptions, so is Swedenborg today classed by many among the theosophists, while in reality he teaches that which is fundamentally opposed to theosophy, in his assertion of the authority of Divine revelation and the absolute and sole Divinity of the historic Christ.

Says Madame Blavatsky (Secret Doctrine, i., p. 28): "The period beginning with Buddha and Pythagoras at one end, and finishing with the Neo-Platonists and the Gnostics at the other, is the only focus left in history wherein converge for the last time the bright rays of light streaming from the æons of time gone by, unobscured by the taint of bigotry and fanaticism." But the same striving after immediate access to the Divine which led Philo Judaeus and the Alexandrian school of Bible interpreters * to seek an inner Divine meaning beneath the letter, and later led the Alchemists to explore nature for the hidden sources of life and the astrologers to read a human lesson in the stars, led also to the abuses of these motives, in

---

* See "Stanley's History of the Jewish Church," Chapter on Alexandria. Also Chapter on Jewish-Alexandrian Philosophy in Ueberweg's "History of Philosophy." i., p. 222.

the sorcery and the black arts. In the Cabala of the Jews, consisting of the two works, the *Jezirah* (creation), and the *Zohar* (brightness), written probably between 800 and 1300 A. D., although ascribed by tradition to a very ancient origin,* ancient Jewish doctrines were modified by the influence of Greek conceptions, especially by the Alexandrians and the Neo-Platonists. The chief doctrine of the Cabala was that of Jehovah creating the world by Divine emanations and the employment of semi-Divine or theurgic agencies intermediate between Himself and the world. In like manner Paracelsus and Jacob Boehme made a mystic study of man as interpreted by the Christian revelation, and the French Saint Simon and the English William Law taught a refined and spiritual doctrine of the inner life and its wisdom which may preëminently claim the title of Christian theosophy. In all these movements, whether of Greek Neo-Platonism, medieval Mysticism, or modern Quietism, we see an effort in relation to the Christian Revelation very analogous to that of Buddha of old in relation to Brahm. Literal tradition and formal priesthood had produced but a sensual blindness and stagnation. The sources must be struck again if a new formation of life was to be opened. The outward was to be cast aside, and access to the inner wisdom attained by man directly.

---

* See Ueberweg. i., 417.

THEOSOPHY AND RELIGION. 39

This was to be had either by direct vision in a state of ecstasy, or by recovering the lost knowledges of the hidden powers of nature handed down in secret traditions of the past, and with these knowledges the very mystic powers themselves of transforming, of healing, if not, indeed, of creating.

It was not, however, until in the present century, through the English occupation of India, whereby the secret recesses of the ancient religion of the east have been thrown open to the curious eyes of western investigation, that the effort was made not only to recover these lost knowledges and powers, but to find an underlying principle of unity between Christianity and the Vedic and Buddhistic systems and to supplant the personal Monotheism of Christianity and Judaism, and we might say of Zoroaster and Brahm, with the impersonal, formless All of Buddha, and to abandon the Christian ethics or ideal of human life for that of Buddhism. This is the distinctive claim of the modern theosophists as represented by Madame Blavatsky and her disciples of the English and American Theosophical Societies.*

---

* "The 'Secret Doctrine' is the essence of Hindu, Zoroastrian, Chaldean, Egyptian religion, Buddhism, Islam, Judaism, and Christianity. . . .

"It aims to rescue from degradation the archaic truths which are the basis of all religion, to uncover the unity from which they all sprung; to show that the occult side of nature has never been approached by the science of modern civilization."

From " The Secret Doctrine: The Synthesis of Science, Religion,

There is on the surface so striking a resemblance between many of the teachings of theosophy and those of Swedenborg, when judged of by name only, that we cannot wonder that theosophists themselves who have not studied Swedenborg, on merely hearing the titles of his treatises are ready to assign him a prominent place in their ranks. But this is no more surprising than that, by the same illusive employment of terms, they adduce Christ and the Gospel as a witness to the truth of Buddha, claiming that Christ was only another Buddha, teaching again the old doctrine. There are those who have written books to prove that Swedenborg also was only a Buddhist risen again. The terms "inner and outer," "spiritual and natural," "divine and human," "literal and spiritual sense of Scripture," "apparent or delusive truths" of the letter and of the senses, as over against the true knowledge of the spiritual man; heaven and hell as states formed by character; the "Ancient Word," or the wisdom of the Ancients, Divinely preserved in the solitudes of Asia; the creation of all things by emanations and through the Divine logos or wisdom; the spiritual nature of man as distinguished from the brute; the conquering of desire; the struggle of the spiritual with the natural, and the despair in temptation, which precede all true

---

and Philosophy," by H. P. Blavatsky, author of "Isis Unveiled," 1888. "There is no religion higher than Truth." Path Office, 144 Madison Avenue, New York.

elevation and illumination;* the promise of victory and peace and light to him that can endure — all these are terms so common to all Theosophists and all New-Churchmen that one could hardly believe that they belong to systems so fundamentally and thoroughly antipodal as these are. If the New Church may be regarded as the latest to appear of all the historic religions, even as theosophy claims to be in essence the oldest, then truly the difference between the two is as wide as the vast stretch of the ages between them.†

That this may be seen we must, therefore, go be-

---

* See especially " Light on the Path," by M. C.

† The following utterances of one of the foreign participants in the Congress of Theosophists, at Chicago, 1893, published in the official journal of the proceedings, will perhaps enable the reader, as well as any brief statement we could select, to judge at once of the resemblances and the differences which exist between the views held by theosophists and the doctrines taught by Swedenborg, especially on the subject of the Sacred Scriptures. At the same time it must be borne in mind that it is one of the fundamental maxims of theosophists that the utterance of no one mind can have any authority for any other, H. P. Blavatsky declaring in her 'Secret Doctrine,' that no theosophic book acquires the least value from pretended authority.

" Scripture addresses itself to the soul and not to the senses. The key to the inner meaning of the Scriptures must be sought through and beyond the outer, in which Revelation clothes itself, every interpretation being sifted and modified, rejected or accepted on its own merits, by the mental faculty. . . . Religion is soul-culture. Revelation is the knowledge requisite thereto. Revelation is an intuition of the Kosmos, which reveals itself in and through the

hind words to the ideas they stand for. Theosophy is indeed a Protean system; it may take on any and all forms, still claiming to be itself; but when it takes on the nomenclature of the theology of Swedenborg, it means something wholly different from Swedenborg's meaning, and this it is important that all should know who desire to know truly either system.

It is customary for theosophy to call itself in the abstract simply "the truth." "It is not religion,"

---

primeval consciousness of mankind. This Kosmic intuition reaches down to and is the voice of Deity."

" The Seven Principles of Theosophy:

" I. It is not in the Literal Meaning that Divine Truth is to be sought.

" II. Oneness of Deity underlying all manifestations.

" III. Duality of Deity in the noumenal and phenomenal.

" IV. Absoluteness of Deity, unchanged by manifestation.

" V. Divinity of man and Humanity of God.

" VI. Law of Analogy or Correspondence, acknowledging unity and duality; enjoining us to seek below that which is above, and to seek above that which is below; to know the macrocosm by and through the microcosm; to attain universal wisdom through self-knowledge.

" VII. All Scriptures are therefore esoterically true, and falsified only exoterically by the imperfect natures of the personality through whom they are revealed. All saviours of men are 'Christ,' although they may not know His name.

"The first chapters of Genesis are: I. An account of the creation of earth. II. An account of the creation of the first four races, our ancestors as described by Mrs. Blavatsky. III. The generation and emanation of the soul from and by the Seven Potencies and Hierarchies of God. They it is who say 'Let us make man in our image.' The Hebrew books are, besides the history of the Hebrew nation, a symbol of the history of the soul. Egypt is materiality; Canaan is

says Madame Blavatsky, in her "Key to Theosophy," "but the truth underlying all religions." It would seem as if so broad a system as this ought, if it be genuine, to truly occupy some sublime height to which all could look up, and from whose point of vision those of separate and more limited faiths could properly range themselves in their respective subordination and dependence. But do we find this so in the theosophy whether of Buddha or of Madame Blavatsky's Secret Doctrine?

---

passional and sensuous nature to be subdued by Israel, a soul-seeking regeneration. This Promised Land is the Kingdom of Heaven.

"In the Gospel the events in the life of Christ represent the inwardness of the soul, its Divinity, its evolution, regeneration, and reincarnation." (Miss Muller of London. Address on Theosophy as found in the Scriptures Hebrew and Christian. Congress of Theosophists. Chicago. 1893.)

See also the following description of the state of those who are "no longer concerned with history," and who, perhaps, on this account assume the assumption of the Virgin Mary and her immaculate conception as historical phenomena like all others in the "process of evolution," serving only to symbolize the progress of the souls of the illumined.

"For those thus initiated the mind is no longer concerned with history; the phenomenal becomes recognized as illusory — a shadow projected by the Real. One thing is and abides — the soul in man — mother of God, immaculate; descending, as Eve, into matter and generation; assumed, as Mary, beyond matter into life eternal. One state, supreme and perfect, epitomizes and resolves all others — the state of Christ, promised in the dawn of evolution; displayed in its process; glorified at its consummation. To realize the assumption of Mary, to attain to the stature of her Son, these ends and aspirations constitute the desire of the illuminate." (The Perfect Way. Preface to the Revised Edition. p. 9.)

Do we find in theosophy a true synthesis? If so what is it in its synthetic form? If it only contains the several truths which in more or less fragmentary forms are found in all religions, then its inventory of these may be useful and convenient for reference, although it adds nothing to our information; but according to theosophy the synthesis of truth is the very abyss of the formless and the ineffable, where the knowledge disappears, and at the sight of which we lose our own identity and cease to be ourselves; of what use then can the synthesis be?

The moment we arrive at the synthesis in distinction from the several definite forms of faith embraced in it, we find ourselves in a nowhere, where all distinctions disappear and where neither synthesis nor thesis of any kind can avail for ought any more. The cycle of its evolution is from nothing back to nothing.

The very opposite of Christianity, which derives the personality of man from the personality of God into whose image he was created, this synthesis of all religions would make God or the All dependent on man for His personality, and this only in transient phases and while under the delusion of distinct existences. The only perfection is in the relapse into the unconscious impersonal All. Nor can this "synthesis" be regarded as a form of truth, for the truth comes as a light into the world, but this is something that secretes itself; that cannot be known except to be found to be unknown; that is understood by only the few and the wise, and they do not understand it; that can assume no definite form while remaining itself; that cannot be taught, because to be taught is to become what it is not; that cannot be seen, because to be seen is to be what it is not. It is eternity; it is silence; it is night; it is not life, for to live consciously would be to die to its eternal and absolute infinity; it cannot make itself known but by illusions, and so when man thinks he knows it he is most deceived of all, and he is only sure of knowing the All when he knows nothing at all. This "All" in becoming a personal God in man only enters into the realm of illusion, so that even God Himself is illusion. I might go on with pages and pages of these subtle antinomies — the cunning jugglery of metaphysical thought as old as philosophy itself. They form simply a phase of the play of the ratiocinating faculty in man, and are in no sense entitled to the claim of being the Divine knowledge or the synthesis of truth.

Somewhere in his writings Swedenborg speaks of the desire he had in his early years to know what God was doing before the creation of the world, or before time began; and he tells us that this kind of questioning would lead only to delirium. I know of no more fitting name than this to give to an effort to found a system of truth and of religion on that conception of Being which regards it as true only when inconceivable and indescribable, and as being untrue and an illusion just in the degree that we know of or say anything about it.

If any one will read the substance of both ancient and modern philosophy, including the deepest thought of Plato and of the Vedas, as well as that of Spinoza, Kant, and Hegel, regarding the relation of the absolute to the determined, of the "Be-ness" of the theosophists, the formless Being to the Being formed — he will find it in Swedenborg's doctrine of the *esse* and *existere* in the chapter on God the Creator, in the "True Christian Religion." There[*] he will find the discussion presented in the enduring form of reason itself, not in the strange pictures of a delirium. The law that governs the relations of the Divine Esse, Existere, and Procedere, is not merely the abstract fact of action or reaction with nothing to cause either the action or the reaction, but it is the universal and fundamental law of all being and all creation, the law of the Discrete Degrees, End, Cause, and Effect: end producing cause, and end and cause realizing themselves in the effect. And this End is not an abstraction — not an "eternal silence breathing" — it is so real and Divine and living a thing, nay, so Divinely human a thing as love; and this Cause is so Divinely powerful and fair a thing as

---

[*]Also, more particularly, in the work on the "Divine Love and Wisdom," Parts III. and IV.

wisdom ; and this Effect is a finited world of uses, in which the very delight of life is experienced.

How different from the world created by the formless All of the theosophist. This formless, eternal *Be-ness*, unmoved, or without will, breathes itself awake and becomes, according to Jamblicus, a Being but not a being somewhat ; next it stirs itself into the Being of the Good, the Supreme God of Plato ; then into the Being of Wisdom, the logos or reason thinking a world ; then into a second logos, or logos creating a world ; then into the logoi, or many agencies such as archangels and other powers of the air. We follow this descent of the formless all down into the world of matter, which is the world of separateness, of distinctions, of individuality, and personality. Here all is strife and misery and unhappiness because of the sense of want, of incompleteness, of desire, that comes from things being apart that belong together. The only way to overcome this misery of life, of being awakened from the eternal slumber and night, is to go back to that slumber, to go back to this unity — this sense of all as one. The spirit as man on earth must cultivate the spirit of brotherhood and must overcome all sense and love of self or of one as different from another. The whole object of life is to find that their separateness is an illusion ; that we are all nothing as individuals, and in learning this to learn that all pain and sorrow, coming from this illusion of life, is really nothing. And why not then also to learn that all that we hold as true, whether as pupils or as masters, is equally illusion and nothing? and so theosophy with the rest. All life is essentially an evil because thus made up of the sense of individual personality; brotherhood consists in learning to know that this individual personality is an illusion and that all are one and the same; the escape from the evil of life is in coming into this sense of the wholeness — the being and knowing one's self as the all.* Those that have lived many lives on this earth through successive incarnations, have learned more of the universal life by overcoming more of the illusions; these are the wise ones, the great souls, and adepts — the masters. When they, through successive incarnations, can overcome no more illusions on earth, they die finally and go to heaven or enter into a state above the separateness of the material world. Here they enter again into the sphere of the logos, even the first logos. They are gods; they are in the bliss of universal knowledge and universal power. They have attained to the pure vision of themselves as God. Some of them, however, are not content to remain in this heaven, but after a resi-

---

* The ethics of theosophy is brotherhood; and brotherhood with man and with beast. And this is based on the doctrine:

"Man thou art not alone. Thou art one of millions of existing beings; because thou art God and they are God. God pervades the whole universe and the universe itself is God." (Chakravati. Chicago Address. 1893.)

dence there of some fifteen hundred years these wise ones return to earth and live in retired places to teach in secret this Divine knowledge to the few who are prepared to receive it, and so to afford the advantage of their manifold experience of living to others who are laboring under the illusions of life and its evils. These are the great souls or the Mahatmas.* They are practically omniscient and they work their will as demiurges among men. They are the masters

---

* " There exists a perfect knowledge of spiritual things. This body or system of truth has been discovered by perfected men, not only discovered but verified over and over again, building a great system; nothing has been allowed to stand except what has been experimented upon, redemonstrated by generations of seers; so that the very truth itself should lack no means of demonstration, more complete than any known to Western science." (Mrs. Annie Besant. Address before Theosophic Congress. Chicago. 1893.)

The above emphatic acceptance of the authority of tradition and the demonstrability of the truth stands in strange contrast with the general position of theosophists that each man is the only standard and only revealer of truth to himself. But this is again modified by the claim made by the writer further on of the ability of every one to attain to the immediate vision and knowledge of the absolute Spirit.

"Only those whose will is strong, who for life after life have learned to conquer the material and the intellectual and so developed the spiritual faculty, only these have power to discover, to prove, to verify. But in that every man is Divine; in that Divine love is your heart and mine; therefore we can also feel the pulses of the spiritual life urging us to the realm of the Spirit, and just in proportion as we feel them, the vision begins to open until we know of a certainty that spiritual truth is real and not a fable." [Applause.] (Mrs. Annie Besant. Chicago Address. 1893.)

from whom the theosophic societies of America and England derive their knowledge — not directly, but mainly through Madame Blavatsky, who was taught by them directly and who has handed down the teaching of these immortal prophets in her " Secret Doctrine."*

But the possible destiny and career of man does not end with being a God in the other world, nor a Mahatma, or god incarnate, in this; after that sense of being one with all humanity, that absolute brotherhood which is reached in feeling one's self to be them all and them all to be one's self, which is the feeling that one is God, then this last illusion must be overcome; for this feeling of being something, even a god, is in so far a feeling of separateness or of distinction; even this must be lost ere the ideal perfection — the absolute unity — is reached. So even the sense of godhood is lost and with this last illusion dispelled the spirit falls back into the eternal night, silence, and slumber — the formless all.†

Such is the circle of life as depicted in the writings of the reorganized teachers of modern theosophy. A

---

* "Helena Petrovna Blavatsky, to whom many of us owe our very knowledge of the life of the soul, whose memory we revere more than the memory of a mother, for the mother gives life to the body; the spiritual teacher awakens the soul; yet no authority is claimed for her, only gratitude. We know no division; we have learned to transcend it." (Mrs. Annie Besant. Chicago Address. 1893.)

† See "Light on the Path," by M. C.

religion of the elements, it might be called, rather than of man.*

The only really ethical feature in theosophy would seem to be in the bearing of this doctrine on the conduct of life. It is true the study of comparative religion is emphasized as one of the chief objects of the Theosophic Society, and this with a view to observing that all religions are but phases of one, all faiths are but the varied phases of one truth; but when this underlying truth is found to be the truth that all so-called truths entertained by men are alike illusions, that life formed by these truths however excellent is an illusion and an evil, and that the end of all learning is to know the bliss of not knowing, we can hardly see that this object of the Society has much practical value beyond the doubtful one of making one feel indifferent toward all professed and defined forms of faith. As the motto of the society is "The highest religion is truth," we can understand how the idea of brotherhood and brotherly love is attained — not in any personal affection, or even personal service or devotion, but in the simple knowledge that we are all one and the same spirit, strug-

---

* "From Para-Brahm, the highest spirit, came forth the two — Parusha=spirit, Prakreti=matter — two different facets of the Om which exists behind all illusions. The electricity of the positive and negative is hence derived. Parusha is the positive, Prakreti the negative; when these come together there is the spark of the universe — the spark of the individual mind." (Chakravati. Chicago Address. 1893.)

gling back from the evils of the waking life of separateness into the bliss of slumberous unity. Love, as ministering to another's delight, or even to his relief from misery, can at most only reveal the death that lies in the cup of every normal pleasure of earth, and that shows to the sufferer that he is reaping only what he has sown. But as life is an evil, because of the separateness of the personalities here, therefore brotherhood itself is an evil, since it could not exist without separate personalities. The object of life being thus reduced to getting rid of the evil of being a person apart from others, the only ultimate object, or object beyond life, would be to be lost in the sense of an absolute self. And if this is bliss as opposed to the misery of the individual personal life, then it must be the bliss of infinite self-love. The "holy mission" of the Mahatmas in teaching this doctrine of the evil of personality, cannot be regarded as holy by any to whom the doctrine of Divine Love appeals as it is set forth by Swedenborg and declared by him the fundamental doctrine of Christianity and all real religion. This doctrine declares God the Eternal to be a Being of essential Love, Wisdom, and Use, forever the Divine Man and the one Divine Person. As Infinite Divine Person He loves, and from love by His wisdom He creates objects of His love, and He creates an ultimate plane of being where, in their utmost remoteness from Him and separateness from Him, they may most intensely realize not only His love to them as not Himself, but also most freely reciprocate their love to Him as not themselves. Love, says Swedenborg, desires its good and its delight in another, and creates another in order that it may be the receptacle of its good and experience its delight. Earth and the life of earth is made to be the field of the delights of God, and God is, speaking humanly but reverently, never so happy as when He sees innumerable creatures not merged into Himself nor into one another, but in their most intense sense of individual personality serving one another and desiring that the good of each may be the good of the other. Not only is earth the scene of this multiplicity of individual lives — earth is the material out of which the sense of distinct individuality is built up by the soul born into an earthly body. But that individual form, so acquired through the sensuous life of this material plane, remains with it forever; it is its eternal equipment for manful service of the Lord in the hosts of the blessed. The soul cannot leave this its spiritual body once formed on earth, which has become its very form and personality, to return to earth and take on another form and personality here. Only an impersonal soul, if we can use such a term, would do that, and for a soul to become impersonal would be to die, to lose its identical being once and for all. Our individual personality is the growth on earth of a spiritual body, from the simplest germ up to the full stature of man, according to the growth and development of the physical body; the potency of the full man is in the germ because it is in the life from God there; but for the fully developed man, that is, the spiritual body, to enter actually again into the germ to be born, would be like the oak-tree entering into the acorn to grow again in the earth. Of all the strange misconceptions and assumptions regarding Swedenborg's teachings as resembling those of theosophy, nothing is so unwarranted and so inexcusable a violation of the truth, as the assertion repeated from author to author that Swedenborg teaches the doctrine of Reincarnation, and even that "this doctrine lies at the basis of his entire system." It is equally strange and to be regretted that authors who have been challenged to produce a single sentence from Swedenborg warranting this assertion, have admitted their inability to do so and yet allow their statements to stand uncorrected. It is only because, we may suppose, of the wide misconception that Swedenborg's doctrine is, in general, in harmony with theosophy, whereas not only here but in other essential points, they are, as I have said, entirely unlike. For, to take another instance, heaven, or the end of creation, far from being a mere relapse into slumber, is, according to Swedenborg, a perfected human civilization — a vast society of regenerated men and women living in the enjoyment of perpetual youth, serving God as the vehicles or instruments by which the Infinite Divine Love and all its delights are communicated in service one to another, and as ministering spirits to those in spheres below, even to man on earth. Life on earth, far from being an evil, is a casket filled with rare jewels to be opened and enjoyed every day anew, and death is the gate into a life of the varied activity of human usefulness belonging to a spiritual world, and affording more and more happiness to all eternity.

I have spoken above of that ethical nature among theosophists which may be regarded as constituting their religion, but the question arises whether there can truly be any religion without a belief in a personal God. The religion of idolatry, of Animism in all its forms, of practical or popular Buddhism, worships and prays to something outside of self as having a power to bless or to protect from harm. The Christian prays to his God within, but not to himself. But Madame Blavatsky, in answer to the question, "Is there a personal God," says "There is not;" and to the question, "Shall a man pray," she answers "No; why should he;"* and the explanation that the only personal God to whom a man could pray is the man's higher self, and that in this sense Christ prayed to the Father in Himself, only shows that, to the theosophist, man's only God is his higher self, and every man is a Christ.

---

* "A Key to Theosophy." H. P. Blavatsky. The Path Office. New York.

It is in this doctrine of the higher self that we reach the test of the practical worth of theosophy as a religion. Since the expulsion from Eden the will of man with its larger and larger accumulation of hereditary evil, dictates to man what shall be its good, and points out the way of attaining it. To overcome this false good there must be an authoritative doctrine of truth which can say with the voice of God," "Thou ought: thou ought not." This voice comes in. Divine revelation; in the Law and in the Prophets and in the Historic Christ as the Incarnate Word and the Redeemer. But if the only God is our heredity, our reincarnated spirit bearing its burdens and oppressed with its karma or unalterable law of retribution, what authoritative voice can speak to us? "No spirit," say the theosophists, "can teach another the truth." It can point out the path in which one may find the truth in himself. But what truth is *there* but the sound of the voice of his deluded and delusive will? If, on the other hand, one obeys the voice of a Master and looks to him for light and strength, then one surely is adoring a personal God and is praying to him. So is Buddha and so are innumerable Buddhas worshipped; even the little idols, the millions of gods which crowd the temples of these races whose teachers tell us that there is no personal God for man to worship. It is better; it is of the Divine Providence that it is so; for the lowest and deadliest of all forms of idolatrous worship is the worship of one's self as God. As the perverted will of man, subject as it is to all the delusions of evil, and burdened with hereditary love of evil, cannot be trusted to teach the truth, therefore after the expulsion from Eden there were placed at the east of the Garden cherubim and a flaming sword which turned every way to keep the way to the Tree of Life.

The cherubim are the Divine Providence guarding the holy knowledges from profanation by the intrusion of the lusts and phantasies of a perverted will. No more was man to enjoy the immediate vision which belonged to the "man of integrity." The truth that gives life and can save could henceforth only come by the outer way, through the intellect in the voice of the uncorrupted Word. The way to the Tree of Life which is in the midst of the Paradise, is henceforth only opened through the Word as Divine, not through the ecstatic vision of man's corrupted will. "I am the Door," is the word of the Incarnate, the Historic Christ — the revealed, not the inwardly evolved Word. "By me if ye enter in ye shall be saved; he that climbeth up some other way, the same is a thief and a robber."

The vital error of theosophy as a system of religion is, therefore, in this substitution of the individual authority — the Christ that, it is claimed, every man is to himself — for the One, the Only, the Historic Christ, Jesus the Incarnate Word and the Saviour of the world.

If the pure Word could speak as once in man's uncorrupted will, then the voice of God could still be heard in the Garden. But the will once corrupted, it can be born anew only of a nature — a personality — not itself, that of the Incarnate Word. This is why such stress is laid in the Gospel on man's *believing* that Christ is the Son of God and that the Word is to be obeyed. Here is an objective law by which man may control himself; here is a truth which a man may truly call "his Master," and to which he may bid his whole nature to bow in obedience; and more than all, here is One, a mighty deliverer, who, in a nature like unto ours, has conquered hell, not only for His own deliverance, but in doing so, for the deliverance of the whole human race as well, and who, therefore, can say to man in every state of temptation: "Be of good cheer: I have overcome the world." "All power is given unto me in heaven and in earth." "Look unto me and be ye saved all the ends of the earth, for I am God and there is none else." "Come unto me all ye that labor and are heavy laden and I will give you rest." To say to every man that he himself is the Christ that teaches himself the truth and that saves himself, is the worst form of delusion, if one is in earnest about overcoming the evils of himself and of the world. Is not this the fulfilment of the warning: "In that day many shall say I am Christ! Go ye not after them"? For which of the many men and women who thus in these days call themselves Christ, have overcome the hells and put Satan under their feet forever? To say that others have done so, and that we may look to them as to the Wise Ones, the Masters, or Mahatmas for either aid or authority, is to admit that these are as gods to us and that we may pray to them; but this is directly contrary to the theosophic principle that the spirit can only be the Christ to a man as it is seeking its incarnation in himself. And if the spirit has overcome all temptation and become the Almighty in heaven and on earth, and therefore can be prayed to, how is it that it is suffering and in want in our personality again; how can the spirit in one's self teach the truth which shall guide, and overcome, and save, when the very self — the very personality — is all an illusion, and so all its thoughts and all its efforts and all its aims to be this or that, are only illusions and vanity? The Christ, the Redeemer, the world needs and cries out for from the depth of its earth, is that Christ that has overcome the hells and in so doing has been lifted up from the earth, that He may draw all men unto Him. He it is who has led captivity captive and has received gifts of eternal liberty for men.

To deny the Historic Christ, to supersede the written Word in which the Divine Truth, handed down from the beginning, still speaks to man in Law and Prophet and Gospel is, like Buddha of old, to deny the Divine inspiration and authority of revelation, and to seek to find a law unto one's self. Or else it may be that we turn to the prophets, to man himself, for wisdom, rather than to Him who alone at all times " spake by the mouth of his holy prophets."

In the very fact that we are entering upon an age of newly-revealed secrets of mind and of body and of the elemental world, the old temptation comes back which the pedant Wagner, in " Faust," reveals when he says, "I know much. I would know all."* The barriers are broken down which seemed once impregnable between matter and spirit ; what shall hinder our entering in ; our seizing upon the forbidden fruit while listening to the seducing words : " Ye shall be as gods knowing good and evil"? Why hangs the veil before the Holy of holies? why swings the flaming sword before the gates of Paradise? why sing the cherubim forever day and night : " Holy, holy, holy, Lord God Almighty!" why? except that it is of the Divine Mercy and Providence that man may not fall into the slavery of his own evil, but may be guided and governed by a holy law, not himself, a law that may point out the evils he is in and may bring the power of the Divine Humanity of his Saviour down into the struggle of his life in overcoming them. To those who believe in and look to Him in His Word, the power to overcome is promised. He overcame the hells by the power of the

---

* " Zwar weiss ich viel, doch möcht' ich alles wissen." (Faust. Goethe. Sc. I.)

Word, when he repelled the temptation, saying, "It is written." To him that overcometh He offers to give to eat again of the Tree of Life which is in the midst of the paradise of God. He alone for all mankind has entered again the Holy of Holies when, at the uttering of the words, "It is finished," the veil of the temple was rent in twain. He it is whose voice goes out to all mankind : "Blessed are they that do His commandments, that they may have right to the tree of life, and may enter in through the gates into the city."

WORKS CONSULTED IN THE FOREGOING PAPER.

SACRED BOOKS OF THE EAST. Edited by F. Max Muller.

VEDIC HYMNS. Vol. XXXII., Part I. F. Max Muller. Oxford: 1891.

THE SAME. Vol. IV.

THE ZEND-AVESTA. Part I. James Darmesteter. Oxford: 1880.

THE TRUE CHRISTIAN RELIGION. Containing the Universal Theology of the New Church. Emanuel Swedenborg. New-Church Board of Publication, 20 Cooper Union, New York.

THE DIVINE LOVE AND WISDOM. Swedenborg. The Same.

OUTLINES OF THE HISTORY OF THE ANCIENT RELIGIONS. C. P. Tiele.

THE BOOK OF THE DEAD. Translated from Pierret's *Livre des Morts*. 1894.

ORIENTAL AND LINGUISTIC STUDIES. W. D. Whitney. New York: Scribner. 1873.

HISTORY OF RELIGION. F. Max Muller.

ANCIENT FAITHS AND MODERN. T. Inman, M. D.

The Secret Doctrine. The Synthesis of Science, Religion, and Philosophy. By H. P. Blavatsky. Office of *The Path*. New York.

Theosophy Simply Put. By a New York Newspaper Reporter. Office of *The Path*. New York.

Light on the Path. By M. C.

The Building of the Cosmos: and Other Lectures. By Annie Besant. Madras: 1894.

A Key to Theosophy. By H. P. Blavatsky.

Report of Proceedings of the Theosophical Congress. World's Fair of 1893.

Theosophic Correspondence. Saint-Martin and Kirchberger. Exeter. England: 1863.

Man: His True Nature and Ministry. Louis Claude de Saint-Martin. London: 1864.

Articles in Encycl. Brittanica: Theosophy. Jacob Boehme. Paracelsus. Cabala.

A History of Philosophy. Ueberweg. New York: Scribner. 1872.

The Perfect Way: or, The Finding of Christ. By Edward Maitland and Anna (Bonus) Kingsford. From the Third London Edition. Lovell & Co. New York: 1889.

THE RIGHT AND EXERCISE OF OWNERSHIP

JULIAN K. SMYTH

"WELL," wrote Robertson the great English preacher, "I care very little for the progress of society, if that only means that some centuries hence, individuals will eat, drink, and sleep more abundantly and more cleanly than the masses now, those individuals being mortal, perishable, and dying out forever. They take away all that makes humanity grand, and then ask you to care for it and its progress. I care for religion — for the hope of *a Church;* that is, a society more united in each other, because more united in God. But separate from that, and the possibilities of nobleness which that involves, the destinies of the race appear to me little more interesting than the contemplation of a tray of silk-worms, obscure and crawling reptiles, which may hereafter become moths, and die when the eggs are only laid."

This view of man and of society, and the way in which they should be studied, seems to me just, not from any sentimental reasons, but because a true classification of any organism is one of the first requisites to obtaining a true knowledge of it. In comparing two objects, the man of science, we are assured, cares nothing about their relative beauty. "For no fundamental distinction in science depends upon beauty." * Are they organic or inorganic, are they living or not living?—this is what he must first ascertain, and by so doing gain his true standpoint.

A little box of earth, examined under a lens, shows it to be full of small, glass-like objects fashioned into beautiful six-sided prisms capped at either end by little pyramids modelled with more than Egyptian skill.

Another little box reveals a quantity of small glassy objects, of the same material chemically; but the angles of the six-sided prisms have disappeared, and all these tiny objects follow curved lines, and appear like a vast collection of microscopic urns, goblets, and vases, richly ornamented and fashioned into the most faultless proportion.

What makes the difference? Not their beauty; for both are beautiful. Not simply their shapes; the distinction runs deeper than that. They belong to different worlds. For the first are crystals, the others are shells. The first belong to the inorganic, or not-living world; the others belong to the organic or living world. The crystals can easily be repro-

---

* Drummond's "Natural Law in the Spiritual World," p. 372.

duced by chemistry; but no chemistry on earth can make one of those tiny shells.*

If it is important to classify bits of glass in the earth in order that we may know their nature and their history, how much more essential must it be that we shall study man, whether individually or socially, under a true classification? If we study his movements as if he were mortal and terrestrial, then in case he is essentially immortal, we are doing no better than if we were to study and account for those tiny shells under the supposition that they belonged to the inorganic world of crystals.

Man is largely studied in this way. His social conditions and needs are studied as if he belonged wholly to this earth. Revelation may be said to be that system of knowledge which makes known the kingdom to which man essentially belongs, and studies him under that classification. Its study or knowledge of God, leads to the study of man, the secret of whose nature has been declared to consist in the fact that he, man, was created in the image of God.† It insists that if this be true, it involves a new classification. It points out that there is nothing which so entirely distinguishes man from the highest animals, as certain powers of thought and feeling which are supernatural or spiritual. And these spiritual powers culminate in one thought and one affection, which

---

* Drummond's "Natural Law in the Spiritual World," p. 372.
† GEN. i. 27.

are as different from anything which an animal feels as the shells of the organic world are different from the crystals of the inorganic world — and that is, *the thought and the love of God.* That is not a matter of sentiment; it is not altogether a question of goodness. First of all it is a question of *fact.* Let men account for it as they will, let them try to trace its development from mere animism, let them criticize or ridicule the ways in which man has thought of and loved his God, here is the exercise of a spiritual power which indicates the existence of spiritual faculties, which man alone has. You cannot think or love that for which you have no corresponding faculty. An animal cannot think of or love God, for the simple reason that it has no faculty for doing so. It is not a question of right or wrong. An animal simply has not the necessary spiritual equipment or apparatus. It can love its food, it can love the place where it dwells, it can love its kind, it can love its master, the mother can love her young. But there it stops. And it stops for the want of higher degrees of intelligence and love. It cannot love a book, it cannot love abstract qualities such as justice, purity, disinterestedness, not from lack of education but of equipment. Man, however, has the equipment which the animal lacks. He certainly can, if he will, do that which no highest animal can do; he can think of and love God. And this, I say, requires that apart from any question of sentiment, a new classification be made for man. He certainly belongs to another kingdom. This power to think of and love God differentiates him from every other created being. It is so different, it is so unique, that we must in all fairness regard and acknowledge it as his chief or distinguishing mark. So that it is no merely fanciful idea when revelation declares of perfected men in that higher kingdom to which they essentially belong, that they have the name of God written in their foreheads.* That is what marks them as completed or perfected men. That is the purpose to which, judged by their highest achievement, they evidently are fitted. And if, as Mr. Herbert Spencer declares, we are to "call that good which is fitted to the purpose for which it was intended," we are in reason bound to say, that scientifically, manhood, whether individually or collectively, is good whenever and wherever the name of God is written on its broad forehead.

How perfectly this higher nature of man has been exemplified to the human race, no one will fail to consider who carries in his memory the recollection of the Son of Man. For in Him this truth reaches its highest objective manifestation. And although the perfection of His nature is infinite, while man's is finite, yet all the more perfectly does He reveal the relationship which should exist between Divinity

---

* REV. xiv. i.; xxii. 4.

and humanity, and all the more certainly and authoritatively does He claim for man his true classification as the child of God.

It is with this thought of man as a being who is essentially spiritual, and whose life in this world is intended as a means for the beginning of a spiritual development which is to go on forever, that I ask you to consider some of his responsibilities.

Among those responsibilities is one with which his brief earth-life is much concerned, namely, that of ownership or possession. It is a serious subject; for rightly considered it involves the fundamental laws of being. It is a pressing subject; for the exercise of ownership is much abused. I know that most persons are chiefly interested in particular phases or applications of this subject, such as the ownership of land, of machinery, of the accumulation of wealth in the hands of comparatively few. Socialism, with its demand that land and capital, which are claimed to be requisites of labor and the sources of wealth and culture, should be placed under social ownership and control; coöperative production, involving coöperative distribution and the establishment of productive coöperative enterprises; "land-nationalization," or making over the ownership of land to the State, and either raising the land tax so as to absorb rent,* or paying over to the State the whole increase of rent

---

* Henry George.

due to the collective progress of Society, rather than to the individual efforts of the proprietor *—these are some of the special projects growing out of this general subject of ownership, in which many are taking such a strong interest. Their consideration, however, as purely economic questions, is not the purpose of this address. However useful such considerations may be, and however important it may be to know the facts which become established through such considerations, it is equally important that we should study the Divine law and intention with reference to this and similar problems. To attempt such a study, to understand if possible the ethical and spiritual nature of ownership is, then, the purpose of this paper. It is time that we took the position firmly and confidently, that in looking for the highest law of conduct, we should not simply look into what is past and below us, nor even into what is present. Neither should we accept the laws of evolutionary science as our only or chief masters. Without ignoring the past or the present, without overlooking the conditions through which atoms, and the various kingdoms of nature, together with man himself, have passed, we are to look to what is above and before us. Certainly an evolutionary process has been going on. There has been movement, development. The reverent student of nature and of history rises from his

---

* J. S. Mill.

studies with the cry of wonder and thanksgiving on his lips, "God has surely been in the past." But Christianity bids us believe in a God " who was, and who is, and who is to come." It points to Him who is not simply in the first things, but in the last things as well. He was not simply successful in their beginnings ; He will be as successful in their ends. And there is ground for confidence in remembering that the Son of Man proved His omniscience by not staking the truth and the success of His Gospel upon its immediate acceptance and realization, but with His eyes fixed upon future generations, seeing the changes which must come, said with a calmness and certainty, that belong to truth : " Heaven and earth shall pass away, but My words shall not pass away."

It is in this spirit of confidence that I desire to bring to your minds what I understand to be the truth of the Gospel concerning Ownership.

I. The basis of Ownership.
II. The right of Ownership.
III. The exercise of Ownership.

I. WHAT IS THE BASIS OF OWNERSHIP?

The basis of ownership is in the fact that God has made it possible for each man to have a conscious being of his own. He has not simply made each man separate from every other man ; He has made each man conscious of his separateness from every other man. He has made it possible for every man to say "I" and "Thou," with a consciousness of the difference that is indicated by these two terms. The plants are separate; no two blades of grass, it is declared, are in every respect alike. But they are not conscious of their distinctiveness. The members of the animal kingdom are each separate from the other; yet we can hardly suppose that even the highest mammalia reflect upon the distinction between "I" and "Thou," or are in any way concerned to understand the cause or the meaning of the individuality which specializes their life. And yet, unconscious as are the members of these lower kingdoms of this distinctiveness, it is a fact which is essential to them all, and which is most jealously guarded.

Nothing is more wonderful than the way in which, whether consciously or unconsciously, every living organism guards and maintains its being, its selfhood, its ownhood, whatever the stress and strife amid which its life is carried on. The characteristic marks and traits of an organism may be greatly modified; but only very gradually, and after many generations. It is beyond the power of any known force in nature suddenly to overcome, or take away, or transform that "I" by virtue of which it has its existence. You may cut off its nourishment, you may screen off the light, you may deny it heat, you may, in short, make existence impossible; but while life lasts you cannot make a rose yield its rose nature and become, for example, a violet. It will live and die a rose. Men cannot gather grapes of thorns, nor figs from thistles. That is a standing miracle in creation. And if we ask for the origin of this fact, consider whether it is not disclosed in that first announcement or self-description which God made to Moses in answer to the desire to know the Divine name: "I AM THAT I AM." "Thus shalt thou say unto the children of Israel, I AM hath sent me." At the centre of the universe, at the beginnings of its life, is this Divine Individuality, this Divine Ownhood, this Life, this Existence, this Force which does not simply create, and vivify, and preserve in orderly arrangement, but as a first requisite says, "I." Because of this Divine Individuality, this "I" in whom is "no variableness nor shadow of turning," creation proceeds. Creation proceeds, and preservation follows.

I hold it, then, to be essential to right thinking to observe that Revelation makes God known not simply as self-existent life from whom all things proceed, but that it makes Him known as a Divine Individuality; a Divine Individuality who speaks of Himself as "I"— always "I," always individualized, always distinct from the objects of His creation.

Without this Divine Individuality, creation would be impossible; or if possible, it would be without any conceivable purpose. If things simply are, because they are, that is, because they happened, God is no more to be reverenced or praised than if He were some powerful dynamo somewhere at the centre of things, and merely charging them with a purposeless energy which set and kept them going. Even this does not explain what these "things" which the dynamo quickens, are, nor how they came to be, nor what they are intended to do, nor how they gained their distinctiveness from the dynamo itself. One reasons hopelessly from such a beginning. But it is not necessary. There is this other way. At the very centre of things is a Divine Individuality, which, in the consciousness of its uncreated Ownhood, can, and does say, "I AM THAT I AM." Love, wisdom, power (for we see manifestations of these things), individualized in One who says "I AM." God, then, as a Divine Individuality, creates. For Love demands an object which it can love. It is the nature of Love to give of itself to others. "I," if love fills its heart, demands something which it can address as "Thou." It must be separate from itself, else the love for it will be essentially a love for self. Here is the pitfall of pantheistic thought, of which there is so much today. It makes Love simply love itself, and makes God infinitely self-loving. How could this satisfy Love? Love, the life, which cries "I," longs for something other than itself, capable of love, needing love, and, more wonderful than all, capable of loving in return. For Love is not satisfied until in the heart of that which it loves, it awakens a response, and creates a relationship so free and friendly, that it can lavish its blessings upon its willing recipient. But for this, it is conceivable that a world of flowers would have answered the demands of Divine Love, provided God loved flowers. Or a world of singing birds, provided He loved singing birds. Or a universe filled with comets, provided He loved comets. But the flowers know not who toils and spins for them; the birds know not by whose bounty they are fed; the comets know not who gives them their motion. Love can make none of them rejoice. Had they consciousness and speech, they might each cry "I"; but they have not that spiritual consciousness which would enable each to say, "I love the Love that blesses me," nor the freedom which would prompt each to say, "I desire to act in harmony with that Love, and so become a means of blessing to others."

Love must have an object.

Love must have an object other than itself.

Love must have an object other than itself, which can reciprocate that love, act in harmony with it, and become filled with a similar desire to be of use to others.

Behold, then, the wonderful drama of creation as it now begins to unfold itself to our view!

In the beginning, Love, Wisdom, Power, or Use in potency, individualized in One who declared "I AM THAT I AM." Love goes forth robed in Wisdom, strong in the capacity for service. Why does Love go forth? To bring into existence something other than itself, that it may give of itself to something, some one. How the Divine Love, by means of the Divine Wisdom, creates from its own infinite substance that which shall be other than itself, cannot be fully considered at this time. Yet the thought may be presented that Love radiates from itself as a source; it actually projects itself by its own centrifugal force, towards that which is beyond, forming, so to say, an emanation or sphere, which, radiating on and on, may be conceived of as proceeding, and yet becoming separate, from its original love-source. And then by a law of gradations, now for the first time fully set forth in the New-Church doctrine of "Discrete Degrees," these first emanations or spheres of love become the causes and centres of succeeding spheres, each more distinctly separated from its original source than the other, each becoming the cause of others still further removed, until by this self-imparted motion of Love going forth as living or primitive substance, planes of substance less living are formed; and succeeding these, planes less and less living: first the spiritual, with its successive degrees of life, until finally a plane is formed where this substance is no longer living, no longer radiates, but is inert and at rest, and instead of having the power of action has to be acted upon. And this substance at rest, this outmost or terminal sphere of that which, in its beginning, was creative Love, motionless, crass, pressed together, is the substance out of which the natural world is formed; a world, which from its sun, through its heat and light, its atmospheres, waters, terminates at last in the dense matters of the mineral kingdom as a base, which shall serve as a reactive plane from which life may now begin to tend upward. And this it does, and according to those gradual, orderly steps and processes, which it is the beautiful mission of Science to make known. First the mineral, then the vegetable, then the animal. And as we go from one kingdom to another, we keep seeing more and more the triumphs of creative Love. For what was the original end or purpose of Love? It was to create that which would be other than itself. And here they are in innumerable forms of variety and beauty; not strewn in hopeless confusion, but in the most wonderful, orderly arrangement, and moving in accordance with the great law of Use, by which each organism is fitted for its place, and girded for its special service. And everywhere this individuality, this ownhood, which first we saw in God, is, so to say, bequeathed and defended.

And yet, as we go from one form of life to another, as we ascend from one kingdom to another, nothing seems conscious of its individuality. All have it; none know it. Is, then, the purpose of creative Love attained? Not until there finally appears upon the scene a class of beings fitted to receive two gifts — Liberty and Rationality, by means of which a consciousness of individuality can be given, together with a knowledge of the relationship which they are intended to bear to Him who gave them being, and a capacity to know that they are Divinely loved, and of being stirred by that Love, and turning towards it, and reaching out to it, and by means of the very love which found a place in their hearts, loving in return.

At the end of how long and strange a journey is this attained? When man can take up the words which God puts into his mouth, and say in intelligence and faith, "I AM hath sent me," he awakens to a knowledge of one of the most stupendous facts in creation. But when, touched by this knowledge, he can say from the heart, "*I love the Lord*," the circle of creation is completed, the labors of Divine Love are crowned with success.

To what, then, have these considerations led us? "The earth is the Lord's and the fulness thereof"— does not that settle the question of ownership in land? "The world and they that dwell therein"— does not that remove all claims to possessing anything in this world; our bodies, our very selves even?

Is there, then, no ownership but Divine ownership? Is it the Divine intention that we shall say of nothing — our homes, our raiment, our occupations, "It is mine?" Since life is His, has any one a right to say, "I," even? Is not that the prerogative of God alone? "I AM THAT I AM." And was not that reaffirmed when, as the Word made flesh, He said, "Before Abraham was I am." But do you not remember another word of His — and it will clear up the whole difficulty — "As the Father hath life in Himself, so hath He given to the Son to have life in Himself." * The Father is the Divinity Itself from Whom all things are; the Son is the Humanity which was assumed and by means of which our Lord appeared in the world and took the position as of a man among men. And this saying of the Son of Man, although it has its special or Divine application, also teaches the wonderful truth that it is not only possible, but Divinely intended, that every man shall have an individuality, derived, yet separate from God.

Here, now, is a mighty principle. Here is a most important fact to know. I go further and say, that to refuse that fact, to close our eyes to the fact that God has created us with an ownhood or individuality forever separate from His, and to entertain the thought that inmostly we are a part of God, is one of the subtlest and most dangerous delusions that can take possession of the human mind. God can indeed say "I AM THAT I AM." But Paul was right when he said, "By the grace of God, I am what I am." † "By the grace of God," by the Divine permission and intention. It is not necessarily humility to say, "I am nothing." It is not righteousness to try to efface self, and wish for final absorption into Deity. That is simply going in the face of all that God has

---

* JOHN v. 26. † 1 COR. xv. 10.

done. On the other hand, it is foolishness and mockery to say, "I am sufficient unto myself. I, I alone do this, and I do that." We were created. We were created with an ownhood which might in freedom and from reason act in harmony with the life of God, acknowledge that everything good and true which we receive is from Him and not of ourselves, and so be able to say with the apostle, "By the grace of God, I am what I am."

Have I made the truth at all clear? Since God has created man with an ownhood, the exercise of that ownhood in ownership is right. It is true that in this, as with his own nature, man is dealing with what God has provided. The materials out of which he builds his houses, or weaves his garments, or with which he carries on his trade, are not his. They were created. He has simply acquired them, collected them together, or put them to some use. But as with his ownhood, so with his ownership, he is allowed this exercise and expression of his individuality, not that he may act contrary to God, but with Him; and include in his nature that which he may see so perfectly expressed in the Divine Nature, namely, *the love and capacity for use.*

II. THE RIGHT OF OWNERSHIP.

I realize, however, that on this subject of the right of ownership more needs to be said. There is no denying that under our present social conditions, many find it exceedingly difficult to earn a livelihood. The world is as wide as ever; Nature is as bountiful; but the struggle for place, nay the very struggle for life, grows more intense. Thousands of willing workers can find nothing for their hands to do. The relations between the rich and the poor are strained almost to the breaking point. Never was there so much philanthropy. Never, it would seem, were the rich so desirous of helping the poor. The "college settlements" go into the poor districts. Undoubtedly, they help, they serve. Everything that benevolence can think of to brighten the poor man's lot, to care for his children, to bring a ray of comfort or of simple pleasure into his home, is done — willingly done, done at the cost of personal ease. But out of the heart of the world of poverty comes the cry, "We do not ask for your charity; we ask for justice!" For the idea is firmly fixed in the minds of thousands of wage earners that there is injustice. They have been brought to believe that the present social order is wrong. It is difficult for the man in the mines who heaves coal to the earth's surface at what might be called a starvation wage, to believe that his lot should be so different from that of the so-called "coal baron" according to any law of equity. Poverty, too, sees the disclosures of corruption. It sees the shameful use which is sometimes made of wealth. It sees how money is used to influence legislation.

And all this deepens mistrust; it intensifies the discontent. Many lend their ear to the agitator. They become persuaded that they are wrongfully oppressed. They look upon the rich as in some way their oppressors.

With the more thoughtful, however, this mistrust and discontent are not directed against individuals, but against our present social system. For the fact is recognized that our present views and usages have descended to us. They are not the rich man's invention. He, like every other man, receives them as something which has come down to him. And for their descent, be they just or unjust, wise or unwise, he is not to blame. The real question is, Are our present ideas and usages as to proprietorship right? Certainly in the patriarchal system, as has been pointed out, wealth and rule went together. The father of the family and the head of the tribe was the one in whom proprietorship centred. But the patriarchal age has passed away. The principle of the freedom and equality of the individual has come in. And it is because men believe that that freedom is hindered by our social order, that there is such a wide feeling of discontent. The special hindrance of which many complain today, is the ownership of land. The ownership of land which is not used for some purpose, but is simply held for a rise in value, is believed, by an apparently increasing number of people, to be the chief cause of the inequalities and distress which we see; and the remedy offered is to levy a tax on all land that shall equal the annual value of the land itself, irrespective of the use made of it, or the improvements on it, removing at the same time all taxes now levied on the products and processes of industry.*

I state this in almost the exact language of its chief advocate. Thus far it is simply a problem in economics, which men competent to deal with such matters must consider. As a question in economics, the Church has no business with it. The proposed method of taxation may be wise, or it may be unwise and utterly impracticable. The Church's opinion on a point of this kind is of no value. Its office is not to find out how to tax land, but how to live on the earth as immortal men and women. And there would be no excuse for my bringing in this question at all, but for the fact that it is urged as a religious question. The Bible is drawn on for its support. It is based, so it is claimed, on spiritual principles. This world is the creation of God. The men brought into it for the brief period of their earthly lives are the equal creatures of His bounty. Being the equal creatures of the Creator, equally entitled under His Providence to live their lives and satisfy their needs, men are equally entitled to the use of land, and any

---

* Henry George, "The Condition of Labor," p. 9.

adjustment that denies this equal use of land is morally wrong.*

That is the argument. With such propositions the Church has much to do. For between the declaration that the world is the creation of God intended for man's use, and that all land should be taxed at its " site value," there is a wide break. The two things may or may not belong together. The earth is the Lord's and He made it. That truth we believe. But He has given us no revelation as to how it shall be held, or divided, or taxed. Land, it is declared, " is a prime necessity of life." Is it any more so than food? Man in order to properly exist on even the physical plane of his nature, needs land, food, clothing, shelter. Should all these things be provided him? He needs them; he cannot do without them. Are they, then, his by virtue of his need? Is it wrong to lay upon man this necessity of effort for obtaining for himself what he requires? It is confounding things to say that this world is the creation of God, intended for man's occupancy, and that *therefore* men are equally entitled to the equal use of land. To say that because all men need the use of land, the right of proprietorship must belong to all men, that is, to society, and not to individuals, is not, according to any revelation that we have, a Divine requirement. It is not required; it is not prohibited. In this, as

---

* Henry George, " The Condition of Labor," p. 9.

in many other things, mankind is left in freedom. I do not forget the oft quoted words : " The earth hath He given to the children of men." That is a general declaration. God has created the world for man's use. He has set man upon it. He says He has given everything into his hands — the beasts of the field, the fowls of the air, and the fish of the sea.*
That this forbids individual proprietorship of what is acquired through honest effort, is nowhere stated. One of the commandments warns us against coveting our neighbor's house or his field.† This certainly implies individual possession of land. The fact is, the adjustment of all these questions of division or of ownership is left to men. They can determine to hold land in common ; they can agree to hold it as individuals. And I suppose that under either system men can be saved. I suppose, too, that under either system men can be selfish and avaricious. The Church's function is not to devise economic measures. Neither is it called upon to act as judge or divider about temporal possessions. On the contrary it has a right to protest against any effort to draw her into the political arena under the pretence that the question involved is a religious question. The Church should not be deceived. Neither the taxation nor the division of land is a problem that falls within her domain. With every desire to be

---

* Ps. viii. 6, 7.   † DEUT. v. 21.

just, she is not qualified, and was not intended to be, to pass upon matters of this kind. An enlightened political economy slowly learns the laws of social well-being by experience, while true religion, by revelation, learns the living principles of those laws. And so is fulfilled that saying: "Truth shall spring out of the earth, and righteousness shall look down from the heavens."*

There are, however, two important factors of ownership which religion does insist upon: —

1. Everything which, as we say, "belongs to us," is essentially a gift. Primarily, essentially, everything is God's — not lands alone, but our very selves even. "It is He that hath made us, and not we ourselves; we are His people." † Our spiritual faculties, our moral faculties, our physical powers — these are not of our invention or creation. We gain possession of them through use. "A man can receive nothing, except it be given him from above."‡ The declaration that that only is one's own for which or upon which he has expended some labor, is a misstatement. Man's first possession, himself, is something in the creation of which he did nothing. Our Lord plainly said: "I sent you to reap that on which ye bestowed no labor; other men labored and ye are entered into their labors."§

2. It is, however, manifestly according to the Di-

---

* Ps. lxxxv. 11. † Ps. c. 3. ‡ JOHN iii. 27. § JOHN iv. 38.

vine Will that what we have should be for the sake of Use, and not for the sake of selfish possession. The two things, Gifts and Uses, belong together. They reveal and fulfil each other. And all that comes to man rightfully, whether by gift, or through honest individual effort, or through both, God allows him to distinguish by that word MINE.

III. THE EXERCISE OF OWNERSHIP.

The exercise of Ownership — to speak now of our last point — is, then, essentially stewardship. It is not hoarding. It is acquiring things for the sake of use and not for the mere sake of having them. The things themselves, be they houses, lands, talents, knowledges, righteousness, are not of our creating. God has been before us and made their acquisition a possibility. And He has granted this possibility, and even allowed the sense and the right of possession, in order that our natures might act in unison with His, and thus develop into His image and likeness through a life of use. God owns the world. The old thought that He created it for His own glory, makes Him a glory-loving God. He created it for the sake of use. If man, in the exercise of his ownhood, uses his ownership for self alone, he is acting contrary to God and contrary to the laws which God has made operative in Nature.

For Nature shows us on every hand that use is the

true law of life. It is true that Nature has been chiefly read in terms which tell of an individual struggle for life. It is true that one function of every living organism is Nutrition, and that in the exercise of that function it must struggle for food. "Root, trunk, branch, twig, leaf, are to the tree so many organs — mouth, lungs, circulatory system, alimentary canal — for carrying on to the utmost perfection the struggle for life. But this is not all. There is another piece of apparatus within this apparatus of a wholly different order. It has nothing to do with nutrition. It has nothing to do with the struggle for life. It is the flower. The more its parts are studied, it becomes more clear that this is a construction of a unique and wonderful character. . . . Watch this flower at work for a little while and behold a miracle. Instead of struggling for life, it lays down its life. After clothing itself with a beauty which is itself the minister of unselfishness, it droops, it wastes, it lays down its life. The tree still lives; the other leaves are fresh and green; but this life within a life is dead. And why? Because within this death is life. Search among the withered petals, and there, in a cradle of cunning workmanship, are a hidden progeny of clustering seeds — the gift to the future which this dying mother has brought into the world at the cost of leaving it. The food she might have lived upon is given to her children, stored around each tiny embryo with lavish care, so that when they awaken into the world the first helplessness of their hunger is met. All the arrangements of plant-life which concern the flower, the fruit, and the seed, are the creations of the struggle for the life of others. . . . Every plant in the world lives for others. It sets aside something, something costly, cared for, the highest expression of its nature. The seed is the tithe of love, the tithe which Nature renders to man. When man lives upon seeds he lives upon love. Literally, scientifically, love is life. If the struggle for life has made man, braced and disciplined him, it is the struggle of love that sustains him." *

Here, then, in the words of a reverent student of Nature, is the law of Use, according to which the ownhood of man should enter into the duties of ownership. How wonderful it is! How high! how sacred! How telling do those words of the Son of Man become: "By their fruits ye shall know them." And that, in the light of the best science of today, comes to mean, if an organism lives its existence only in this intense struggle for life, if it has not included this other and higher struggle for the life of others in the formation of seeds and fruits, it has failed. It has failed to do and to be what it was intended to do and to be. The fruit is the test. The fruit is the sign of a complete life. If there is no fruit, even the leaves will presently wither away.

---

* Drummond, "The Ascent of Man," p. 227, *et seq.*

Christian revelation proclaims the same law. How clear and how impressive is the law of ownership as set forth in the parable of the talents. The householder brings his talents of gold, and he places them in the hands of his servants. Not to all alike does he give, but to each according to his several ability. He places the shining gold in their opened hands; he makes them the stewards of his wealth; and then he goes away. He goes away, and they are left with their master's riches. They are to make use of this wealth as if it were their own, and yet in the knowledge and acknowledgment that it is his.

God comes, and He gives us talents of various kinds, "to every man according to his several ability." He makes us His stewards. And then to all appearance we are left alone with our talents. He will not take away our ownhood; to all intents and purposes He grants us ownership and freedom in deciding how we shall exercise it. Shall we hoard it, or shall we make it productive? Shall we make it a selfish possession, which we keep guarding, and dreading lest we should lose it; or shall we use it, and by doing so increase both the riches and our capacity as stewards? And it seems from the parable that life itself was judged by the way in which each one in the parable fulfilled the responsibilities of that ownership with which the master invested them. It tested their character. It determined the quality of their life. It was the intended opportunity for a very important development.

The Lord is the Divine Householder. The earth is His and the fulness thereof, the world and they that dwell therein. He has created us, and not we ourselves. But He has created us with an Ownhood, in order that we might seem to live as of ourselves, yet in the acknowledgment that we live from Him. And because of this Ownhood, He has granted us the exercise of Ownership, and has entrusted us with possessions which really are from Him, but which He allows us to hold as if they were our own. And this He does, in order that as of ourselves we may develop a capacity and a love of use. But if we forget that essentially our ownership is stewardship, and that what we have is not for the mere sake of having but for the accomplishment of good, we shall fail. We shall fail to do and to be what He made it possible for us to do and to be. For our Ownership is ever at the hazard of two extremes:

1. It may be carried to excess. Excessive ownership is avarice; and that is divinely condemned. "Woe unto them," it is written, "that join house to house, that lay field to field, till there be no place, that they may be placed alone in the earth!" * That desire for exclusive ownership and control, whether in houses, in lands, or in anything else, is utterly wrong, and bad for the soul. It is spiritually deadening. It makes man an enemy to his fellows, it

---

* Isa. v. 8.

makes him heedless of his God, it makes him think more of his barns and of his goods than of his soul, it involves him in anxieties, and heats him through and through with that lust for riches which renders the Divine truth unfruitful. His ownership, instead of being a blessing to him, becomes a curse.

2. On the other hand there is the danger of a deficient sense of ownership. This appears in the squanderer, the prodigal, the man who takes the portion of goods that falls to him and then flings his patrimony to the winds. He does not remember, he does not care to remember, whose these things really are that he is wasting. He does not restrain himself with the thought that he is using good gifts from God for selfish and base purposes. What is intemperance in drink, or of any bodily appetite, but waste? waste of mental gifts, waste of manhood, waste of life! And it comes in large part from a deficient sense of ownership. It grows out of a failure to realize that we hold gifts from God, that we hold them in order that we may use them wisely, and that we shall certainly be judged according to our stewardship.

CONCLUSION.

To sum up, then, we maintain that inasmuch as God has created man with an individuality, or ownhood, the exercise of ownership is not only divinely permitted, but intended in order that thus man may develop a capacity and love of use; and that whatever falls to man rightfully, whether as a gift or as the result of honest effort, he is allowed to think of and use as his, acknowledging that it is given of God, and entrusted to him as His steward. And I believe that nothing short of this will ever cause men to fulfil their responsibilities justly, faithfully, and for the common good. To attempt to do away with this individuality and substitute communism, is not, as we apprehend it, in the line of Divine order. The fact is often mentioned that the early Christians held all things in common; which is true. But it should also be remembered that they failed. And they failed, as I believe, because in the innocency of their hearts, and in their love for one another, they overlooked the necessity in the Divine economy of every man filling and fulfilling his individual responsibilities, in private ownership. This does not mean the absence of neighborly love, or of any coöperation of one man with another. For in the degree that any man comes into a recognition of the true — and by that I mean the spiritual — significance of his ownhood and of his ownership, so much the more certainly will he recognize and deal justly with the equally sacred rights of the ownhood and ownership of others. This cannot be forced. The most perfect economic system would not of itself prevent men from over-reaching or from selfish waste. That must come from that sense of entrustment which religion tries to inspire. It is possible for men individually or collectively to use this earth and all things in it for selfish purposes; it is possible to use it for the fulfilling of God's purposes. That is the way in which God has given the earth to the children of men.

Our Lord stood in the midst of the world's tumult. Around Him were avarice, riches, poverty, oppression, waste. He stood there in the midst of it all, and He said what will ever express the deepest wish of every man who sincerely desires to serve God and his fellow men: "After this manner pray ye, Our Father who art in the heavens, hallowed be Thy name. Thy kingdom come. *Thy will be done; as in heaven, so also upon the earth.*"

THE DIVINE LAW OF USE AND ITS APPLICATION TO INDUSTRIAL PROBLEMS

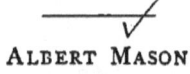

Albert Mason

In the present lecture the term law is used to denote the mode or order in which life operates. Law in this sense has origin primarily in the nature of the Divine Being, and secondarily in the order of creation from Him. Because of this origin, truth concerning the operation of human life when revealed, manifests itself by inherent light. Those who find in the writings of Swedenborg help to a deeper knowledge of the Holy Word, help to so apply its sacred teachings to the particulars of the present life on earth that such life may become effective preparation for a permanent life of usefulness hereafter, can have such help only so far as the truth taught in those writings is clearly seen in its own light. When the truth is thus seen, it no longer rests upon the authority of any teacher. The fact of Swedenborg's mission is best discerned in the truth of his message, and if it is not thus discerned, it were to little purpose to know of his high character, his exceptional learning, or his providential intromission to the spiritual world in preparation for his work.

Varied as may be finite conceptions of the unity of the essential Divine Being and the form of His manifestation to man, there is no school of Christian thought which may not readily accept the teaching that infinite love, the very essence of the Divine Being, uniting with and embodied in infinite wisdom, goes forth and finds expression through infinite beneficent activity — that such is the mode or order in the operation of Divine life, the very law of infinite being. If this central law of life is presented in the teachings of the New Church with greater philosophic distinctness than elsewhere, there is and can be no exclusive property in truth. The one inexhaustible Divine source of truth is accessible to all who sincerely desire to know and do the law, and truth is manifest to each in full measure of willingness and capacity to receive it.

Is this law of Divine life which is written on every page of the Holy Word and shines forth by inherent light to all who will open heart and mind to its reception, merely a grand conception of infinite beneficence which the devout may contemplate and adore in God, but which has no direct practical application to human life? The incessant all-pervading effort of the infinite life to communicate to others the blessedness of its own being, is indeed worthy of the profoundest contemplation, is indeed cause for the most reverent worship and adoration, but such contemplation and adoration serve their highest end by inducing a living recognition that because the law of use is the law of Divine life it is also the law of human life. There can be no true human life save in conformity to this law. The full delight of human living can be attained no otherwise.

No finite conception can adequately measure how far Being which is life itself transcends created being which can be but recipient of life continually given from its infinite source, but the revelation that God created man in his own image is absolute verity. The life given to man is life in the finite degree, after the order and image of the infinite life of the Creator. It does not originate in man, and is not his own in the sense of inherent, independent vitality, but it is given him to be lived as his own and he is endowed with freedom to obey its true order or to pervert it. The law of human living is not affected by the choice of men to obey or disobey. The standard is and must remain the order of human life as given. The law is not a code of regulations to be obeyed under penalty of punishment from a superior for disobedience, but the innate principles of being which determine the felicity of living. Is it not self-evident that the Divine purpose of beneficence in creating human beings to receive the blessedness of living a life after the image and likeness of the Divine, can be accomplished only in the degree in which the likeness to the infinite perfection of the Divine life is attained? Infinite love and wisdom are the essence and substance of the Divine life. Finite love and wisdom received from the Lord are the essence and substance of spiritual life in man. These are not given as reward for applying them to use, nor withheld as punishment for failing to so apply them, but the innate principles of being are such that love and wisdom are nothing save as applied to use.

In "True Christian Religion," 387, it is said:

Love and wisdom are nothing without the good of use. They are but ideal entities; nor do they become real till they exist in use. For love, wisdom, and use, are three things that cannot be separated; if they are separated neither is anything.

Again in no. 375:

Charity and faith are only mental and perishable things, unless, when it can be done, they are determined to works, and coexist in them.

Also in "Divine Love," no. 15:

No man is of sound mind unless use be his affection or occupation.

And in "Divine Love and Wisdom," no. 329:

From the end of the creation of the universe it may appear what use is: the end of the creation of the universe is, that the angelic heaven may exist; and as the angelic heaven is the end, so also is man, or the human race, because heaven consists of the human race. Hence all things which are created are mediate ends and uses in the order, degree, and respect in which they have relation to man and by man to the Lord.

Throughout the writings of the New Church the great law, that faith and love can be preserved and made part of man's spiritual life only through their embodiment in use, is presented in manifold form. Use is the ultimate of the two essential principles of spiritual life, and unless these principles are ultimated they cannot abide in the life. Such is the law of being. Infinite love and wisdom go forth in infinite beneficent doing, and thus use is the law of the Divine Being, and thence of the creation both in general and in minutest particular, and of human life the grand end of creation.

Works outwardly undistinguishable from genuine beneficent living may be utterly without life — may be the embodiment of neither Christian faith nor Christian love. The performance of use for any selfish personal end cannot be of spiritual avail. Use is part and parcel of the Christian life only when it has the two essentials of that life within it. Worthless as it is without these, with them it is that wherein they are manifested in all their power. So far as man individually or collectively lives primarily for himself, he antagonizes and perverts a vital principle of being, and is thereby less a man, less an image and likeness of the Divine Man. Living to himself he loses the genuine human quality of life and the resulting blessedness therefrom which God in loving fatherhood sought to bestow. "For whosoever will save his life shall lose it; and whosoever will lose his life for my sake, the same shall save it."

The teaching that the present life on earth is preparatory to a permanent life beyond, is as old as the Christian Church, but most perverse conceptions of how such preparation is effected have from time to time prevailed. The leading thought of former teaching is gradually passing, and the fleeting shadows of it which remain would be formulated with difficulty from any published creed of the past. Under the new teaching, each individual is determining in perfect freedom the end or purpose of every act, and thereby whether his or her life shall interiorly be in the image and likeness of the perfect life or a perversion of it. Each is determining for himself or herself the degree of conformity or perversion. Under laws of being which cannot be suspended, the measure of conformity interiorly attained in the present earthly living, determines the quality of the permanent living. How vital is the inquiry, Where and what are the opportunities to acquire an abiding habit of useful living? How can we come interiorly and thus permanently into genuine love of use, into the spirit of living primarily for others and only secondarily for self? New-Church teaching is explicit and clear, that the first part of charity is looking to the Lord and shunning evils because they are sins. This is not merely a general truth but a particular truth as well. Not only is looking to the Lord and shunning evils because they are sins, at the very centre of an altruistic life, but it is at the centre of each separate act of true charity. If in the present study our attention is directed especially to the second part of charity, let us not forget that without this first there can be no genuine second. How simple and yet how profound is the following language of Swedenborg:

> He who loves any one fears to do evil to him, for there is a conjunction of souls between them; and hence, in doing evil to one to whom he is conjoined by love, he has a perception in his soul as if he had done evil to himself. Who can bear to do evil to his children, his wife, or his friends? To do evil to them is contrary to the good of love.

To the degree that man is unwilling to do evil to others, and only to that degree, can he will to do them good, to render them service. Only to the extent that, looking to the Lord, he abstains from evil toward the neighbor, can he come interiorly into effort to lead a life of use.

The second part of charity consists in doing good things because they are uses. So-called charity which is of the will only and not at the same time of the understanding is spurious and without strength. If brought into act it is as likely to work evil as good to the neighbor. One who is sincerely obedient to this principle may often seem to a superficial observer cold and unsympathetic toward others, while the truth is, that interior love of use is strengthened by restraining the expression of charitable impulse which the understanding disapproves.

The individual man or woman whom there is occasion to serve is the neighbor, but, in a larger and fuller sense, a society comprising many individuals is such, and the nation comprising many societies is the neighbor in a still larger sense, and the human race comprising many nations yet more fully so. The Church and, in the supreme sense, the Lord, is the neighbor. The good of the individual is properly subordinate to the good of a society, the good of a society to that of the nation, and the good of the nation to the good of the human race, and the good of all is from the supreme good.

The sacrifice of apparent individual good to the real good of a society, a nation, or the race, is in truth the promotion of the highest individual good. A clear conception of the organic character of each collective man aids us to see that the good of parts or members cannot be antagonistic to the good of the larger unit, but the real good of each and all is promoted and conserved by the same unselfish living. If the society, the nation, and the race were mere aggregations of individual lives without organic relation to each other, there could be only monotony of function. It is from the organic character of community life, that the wonderful variety of function or use arises, and thereby a far more perfect life is attainable, not alone a more perfect community life, but a more complete and perfect felicity of individual living. There is an infinite variety of human beings, with as varied capacity for service to others. Each one was created for a specific part in the activities of a heaven of uses, to find in the service for which he was designed his greatest delight of life. In his progress thither, each has some place in this preparatory life which no other can fill as well, and happy is he who finds that place. No two persons being created for precisely the same service, there never has been, and never will be, an exact repetition. No one can find the full measure of delight in any other function than his own.

The ideal life on earth is that which best prepares for heaven — that which brings most of heaven into the soul by bringing the interior life into harmony with that of heaven. It is true that the heavenly quality of life is from the Lord alone, and is never produced by good deeds of men, but the Lord is ever seeking to bestow it, so far as men by looking to Him and shunning evils as sins will permit its reception. Life of heavenly quality, life of use, can become inwrought as individual character, so that it will abide, only as there is effort to bring it forth in the daily acts of this present earthly plane of being. Division of labor is a mark of the descent of heaven to earth, a mark of the progress of civilization in the best sense, not because it has any power to produce a love of use, but because it furnishes the most efficient means of bringing that love into outward life, and thus fixing it as part and parcel of the interior life. Where there is sincere desire to lead a life of use, and clear conception of the means of doing this, labor is loved as a form of use, and the particular phase of it in which the lot is cast is cherished as the form into which the individual love of use can most fully flow, and in which it can find most perfect expression.

It is a grave charge against the present form of social organization, that its normal operation deprives many willing workers of opportunity to serve. There could not well be graver.

This charge is made in all sincerity by numbers who from some cause other than their own choice are deprived of opportunity to have part in the world's active uses, and it demands attention from economists, sociologists, statesmen, and all who directly or indirectly have such relation to the organization of industry as to give promise of effective aid in its reform.

Inadequate return for labor is of itself of minor moment to the laborer, but in its relation to ability to continue and maintain the service it is of the utmost importance. Perhaps to most of those who see in existing social conditions denial of opportunity to many who would gladly serve, insufficient return appears the primary evil involved. As workers we are all prone to give the return or compensation for service undue place. It is not properly the primary end or purpose of service, and there is some recognition that it is not, with reference to more important functions, but it is a most important means to the end, and care should be taken that it be full and adequate to maintenance of the service at its highest efficiency. In the long run, the return or compensation for service will not be less generous and ample, if it be remanded to its proper place as means, and deposed from its usurped place as end.

Inversion of order in the end or purpose of service, is the radical cause of industrial disorder, and no measures of relief are truly curative which do not reach this root of the evil. It cannot be said that the inversion of order involved in serving others primarily for the sake of the return, that is, primarily for the sake of self, is less prevalent with the outwardly prosperous than with those upon whom temporal misfortune presses heavily, nor can the reverse be affirmed. It is not the sin of the employed from which employers are exempt, nor of the latter to the exclusion of the former. The poison infects rich and poor, employer and employed alike, and through all obstructs and hinders the mutual service by which alone the heavenly life of use can be ultimated on earth. Those who can accept Swedenborg's teaching concerning the nature and origin of evil, its overwhelming prevalence at the time of the Lord's coming on earth, the progress of the redemption then commenced, the deep significance of the Lord's second coming in His Holy Word, and what follows thereon, may know by reasonable reflection and rational deduction therefrom, that the industrial and commercial activities of the world are permeated from top to bottom, from centre to circumference, with this destructive principle that self is first and the neighbor second as the end or purpose in life. Those to whom inductive reasoning from observed phenomena is alone convincing, find political economy from its earliest recognition as a science, proceeding upon the assumption that self-interest more or less enlightened, is the actual controlling force in determining the action of men with reference to the acquisition and distribution of this world's goods.

The fact that the Divine law of use has been and is sadly perverted by man, is abundantly established by both methods of reasoning, by the testimony of two witnesses.

Measures for the relief of industrial disorder which are based upon the inverted law of selfish living, are not necessarily aggravation of the evil, but at best can be palliative only. They cannot be curative, because they do not reach the radical cause of the disorder to be removed.

Evils which cannot be removed because of man's unwillingness to put away his own perversity, may be restrained in outward expression by counteracting force in itself evil, and some measure of protection be thereby afforded to others. War is not from heaven, but in origin and quality is from the opposite of heaven. The wars of men never remove the malignant evil from which they spring, but in most wars its destructive manifestation is somewhat restrained by contending force, and nations thereby protected. Strikes, lock-outs, and all forms of hostile action on the part of employers or employed, are of similar origin and quality, and may have similar restraining effect upon aggressive manifestation of selfishness, and thus palliative operation.

It may help us to be patient at the slow progress of outward reform for the correction of industrial disorder, to note that if such reform could outrun the progress on interior planes, it might not aid, but hinder, the permanent interior gain. If secular life has been long and widely permeated with a selfish end or purpose, more or less of what is abnormal and deformed must characterize the social organism. It is of a merciful providence that the laws of being inevitably require that it should be so. Something of protection and of freedom is secured by external conditions which would not be needed and could not exist if the pure heavenly love of use alone found expression in outward order.

If the competitive system of industrial organization is indeed the outbirth of inverted interior life, which may be itself open to question, there is no reason to fear that it would become more mischievous from a change in its animating spirit to genuine love of serving for the sake of the neighbor, while it is obvious that if the animating spirit continued with large numbers to be selfish, the few who had escaped to unselfish living might be defenceless under conditions which were ideal if all were animated by the same heavenly love of use.

No one has cause to bewail his environment who has not advanced beyond it, and he who has some knowledge of his own perversity is slow to assume that he has outrun his fellows in progress toward unselfish living, or that he is aggrieved by their tardy movement. The thoughtful student who observes closely, may well fear that in the present stage of the world's regeneration there is little need or occasion for ideal external industrial conditions. If such need arise, it will betoken an irresistible cause within, certain to produce the desired ultimate.

Those who accept the teaching concerning the redemption which the Lord has wrought in the new age, cannot doubt that the regeneration and reformation of man, individual and collective, will go forward on interior and exterior planes of being, until all shall know the Lord from the least to the greatest. New-Church teaching is plain that the work of regeneration must be a gradual process. It is so from Divine mercy. Interwoven evils, which have become part of the very life, could not be suddenly and simultaneously removed without fatal result. What is true of the progress of regeneration on interior planes, is true to some extent of the progress of reform on exterior planes. The merciful purpose in staying a too rapid or radical overturn was declared on both planes of being.

I will not drive them out from before thee in one year; lest the land become desolate, and the beast of the field multiply against thee. By little and little I will drive them out from before thee, until thou be increased and inherit the land.

Advance in the collective life must proceed upon similar lines to those which it follows with the individual. Sudden radical revolution of industrial organization is neither to be expected nor desired, but steady earnest progress by successive steps, as putting away one evil may aid in the discernment of another.

The largest possible aid which the individual can give to the regeneration of collective life, that it may become interiorly genuine love of use, and the largest contribution which he may make to reform in outward industrial organization, that the Lord's will may be done in earth as it is in heaven, is an earnest personal consecration to unselfish living, not alone a consecration in will and thought, but in effort or act of use, that the heavenly quality may be inwrought to permanently abide in the life.

What are the acts of use by which the individual man or woman can come most interiorly and effectually into the very life of charity, and whereby the largest contribution can be made to the common good? In newly awakened zeal for unselfish living, it is natural to turn for greater opportunity to one or more of the associations with avowed charitable or reformatory purpose. The life of the new age quickens every agency to help those in temporary need, and still more bids Godspeed to all that can confer lasting benefit upon those whom existing social conditions seem to put at a disadvantage.

Those who with efficient organized charity, would visit tenderly and with wise discrimination the literally sick and in prison, have valid claim for coöperation and support in their mission of angelic mercy. An Industrial Christian Alliance seeks to reach men outcast by their own sin and folly, and also to reach other men homeless or unemployed from no fault of theirs, and proves its genuine charity by marked success in imparting to those whom it aids its own spirit of helping others.

College settlements multiply, and through them trained minds and hearts come into close sympathetic relations with those less favored, and study deeply the problems and difficulties which confront toiling thousands. These efforts are prompted by intense longing to serve, and surely something of heaven comes into them.

From Pisgah summits of economic study, leaders are permitted to view the promised land wherein they cannot enter, and with fervor they seek to encourage and strengthen those of their followers who, after long years of journeyings, may lead others to find therein freer access to the natural gifts of God, and peaceful inheritance thereto. The delight of obedient service is not denied to those who in this spirit strive for economic reforms.

All these forms of charity, and many others of kindred spirit, of which these are but typical, are well, and into each and all something of the love of use may and does flow. All who have true love of use can enter sympathetically into the delight of those permitted to have active part in either of them. To some, participation and leadership in these charitable or reformatory activities may happily come as the function or calling in life, and some measure of direct or indirect service for them may be possible to all. The organized activities under the name of charity or reform, are, however, but a small fraction of the service which the world needs and obtains. Increase and perfect every one of them to its fullest measure of efficient use, and neither nor all can become the characteristic life of the community. The more successful any or all, the smaller their part in the continuous common life, until complete success should eliminate them altogether. The great volume of human service to meet human needs, is rendered in the several callings in which individuals are engaged. These varied and interwoven functions are together the life of the community. The excellence or defect of this service is the excellence or defect of the organic collective life. The quality of its animating spirit is the quality of the interior community life. In these functions and by them the community lives such life as it has, and in and by them it must make such advance as it will permit to be made. Reforms in the outward methods of industry, and in the distribution of industrial products, gain in material results, and what is yet more vital, change in the end or purpose of all this busy life which is our environment, must be effected in these several callings and cannot be effected elsewhere.

The common advance is of greater moment than the advance of any individual, but the two are never permanently or really antagonistic. That which gives vigor and efficiency to any part or individual function, contributes to the collective strength of the whole, and the perfection and power of the collective life gives freer scope to each separate function.

If we can see clearly that the common or collective life can come fully into order in outward form and inward quality — can become in each true heavenly life wherein the neighbor is ever first and self second — only as individual workers in the several functions or callings which go to make up that common life shall have come interiorly into love of use and in those functions wrought that love into individual lives of use, then may we see deeper import in Swedenborg's statement that "charity itself is to act justly and faithfully in the office, business, and work in which any one is, and with whomsoever he has any intercourse." The familiar classification of the things of charity comes to us with new force — duties of charity, benefactions of charity, debts of charity, recreations of charity. Is it not clear that there is far more in this order than we are wont to observe? Slight indeed is the attainment which enables us to enter and enjoy recreations of charity, and relatively slight is the impress upon character therefrom. Debts of charity paid from necessity, cannot strengthen the love of the neighbor as acts done from liberty may do. Benefactions of charity are from liberty and are rudiments of charity, serving for initiation or introduction to charity itself, and are its externals. Perhaps in some states of the Church and of an individual man, these mark the limitation of the development of charity, and are as near the central life of charity as the Church or man is willing to go. Duties of charity are the exercises of charity which proceed immediately from charity itself, and in these lies the struggle for life. As these duties of charity, primarily of the employment in which one is and things incident thereto, are faithfully performed in the love of serving, or the reverse, is there success or failure in unselfish living. Our lives are not saved from perversion to selfish ends by occasional or frequent deeds in the name of charity or reform, but if saved at all, are saved in the homely tasks of the every-day life, wherein we may do good to the neighbor daily and continually, and even in the intervals of rest may have the intent and purpose fixed in mind and thereby have the law of use written in the heart.

No study of industrial or economic problems from a New-Church point of view is complete, which does not note the distinct or discrete planes of life. The spiritual life which is within the natural and is its immediate cause, is the permanent life of man and is the life of real value. The natural life is created and exists that it may contain and ultimate the spiritual life during its formative period, and thereby enable the latter to acquire definite and stable quality, but the natural life has not itself value, save as it may thus serve the spiritual. This conception does not minimize the natural life, but gives its maximum worth. The value of the fleeting natural in its relation to the abiding spiritual far transcends any which it could have limited to its own duration. The relation of the spiritual and natural planes is not that of continuous degree, as greater or less in extent, but is distinct difference in kind, as cause and effect. There is continual influx into the natural as effect from the spiritual which is within as cause, but there is not reverse influx of natural effect into spiritual cause. The natural plane affects the spiritual by reaction, to aid and serve, if in obedience and subordination, but otherwise to hinder and impair. No increase or refinement in natural life can make that life spiritual, nor does any development or perfection of spiritual life convert it into natural life. Flowing down or outward upon the natural plane, spiritual life clothes itself with natural life and ultimates itself through it. Close and perfect as is the union of the two by correspondence, they are never merged, never cease to be distinct from each other. Natural truths are distinct or discrete from spiritual truths. We rightly turn to the Church for aid in the apprehension of spiritual truth and the solution of spiritual problems. There have been times and conditions when the Church assumed to speak with authority upon truths of natural science and the solution of secular problems, but the emancipated thought of the New Age does not accept dogmatic teaching in natural science or secular knowledge from wisdom in spiritual things, nor like instruction in spiritual truth from learning in natural science or high attainment in worldly wisdom.

The Church teaches us the law of use and its vital relation to the spiritual life of man, teaches us how the mutual services of the natural life on earth may serve to write the law of use in the heart, but the natural uses of the present life cannot be organized and perfected directly from intelligence in spiritual truths. Natural truths and natural intelligence in them are essential to the efficient organization and prosecution of natural industries. Clear conception of spiritual truths is indeed of great assistance to full apprehension of natural truths in which they must be embodied for application to service of others in the earthly life, but no attainment in spiritual knowledge is or can be a substitute for attainment in knowledge pertaining to things of the natural plane. However clear the individual conception of the Divine law of use, or of the specific spiritual or natural use of the individual calling, however earnest and sincere may be the desire to serve the neighbor therein, there is no escape from the necessity to study the natural truths which pertain to that calling and to acquire natural wisdom in relation thereto. The command, "Thou shalt not kill," is an explicit spiritual law, but it cannot be obeyed on the natural plane, without knowledge of such natural truths as teach what acts would destroy or endanger human life. For its full observance there must be added to never so clear apprehension of the spiritual law, some measure of knowledge in physics and in medical and sanitary science. Every precept of the decalogue must be supplemented by and clothed with truths of the natural plane, in its practical application to daily living on earth.

All service of man to man on earth, is or should be but the specific application of the precepts of the decalogue to the practical affairs of life. In advanced or civilized life the effort to make service of others effective, has given rise to several learned professions and many diversified industries. In each of these is gathered and applied truth exclusively of the natural plane, essential to the full ultimation of the spiritual truth which it is sought to bring into the life through its instrumentality, and each is continually gathering new stores of natural truths, as the interior animating life demands new implements of service.

Statesmen, economists, and sociologists are not less alert than those in other departments of study and activity on the busy natural plane, nor necessarily less responsive to the demands of the inflowing life of the New Age. New needs, arising out of the new awakening of the world's life, are recognized all along the line of its restless activity, and such new needs are met with wonderful rapidity. The trend of industrial organization to more efficient service, is irresistible. The changes already made, numerous and far-reaching as they are, but lead the way for others of yet greater significance. Those who fondly dream that change in industrial organization can be stayed at its present status, have little apprehension of the forces within, which have produced this upheaval. The pain and suffering of the transition period shall pass, but the causes of advance are profound and lasting.

The primary effort toward the solution of industrial problems, is not to discern the mote which mars a brother's vision. Such discernment is not given with sufficient clearness, until there is mastery of the harder task which confronts us at the outset in casting out the beam which obstructs our own.

Not despising or omitting the feasts and recreations of charity, neither avoiding nor withholding the debts or compulsory things of charity, entering gladly and warmly into such benefactions of charity as we may be permitted to have part in, it still remains that the heavenly love of use can be wrought into the collective secular life, can be made an abiding part of the collective spiritual life, only through individual consecration to unselfish living in the homely duties of the every-day work which is devolved upon each.

And righteousness shall be the girdle of his loins, and faithfulness the girdle of his reins.

THE RELATION OF THE CHURCH TO THE STATE AND TO SECULAR AFFAIRS

SAMUEL S. SEWARD

One of the first aims of the sincere Christian, when he awakes to the responsibilities which his new and conscious relations to the Lord impose upon him, must be to apply the Divine truths he has taken as the guide and inspiration of his inner life, to all his outer duties, and especially to the affairs of the state.

Such a man is, as the Apostle says, "a new creature," or "creation." He is "born again," or "from above." He has put off "the old man which is corrupt according to the deceitful lusts," and "put on the new man, which after God is created in righteousness and true holiness" (EPH. iv. 22-24). New spiritual motives from the Lord have taken possession of his heart, and begun to exercise a predominating influence over his actions. Whereas before he did what is right for the sake of the good opinion of others, or of greater success in the world, he is now actuated by a pure and simple love of what is right for its own sake. His will is in harmony with the Divine will.

Loving what the Lord loves he receives the Lord's love in his heart, and desires to act from it in all that he does. He is full of the spirit of service. He loves to do good to his fellow men — even to those with whom he is most remotely connected. He feels a love not his own — higher and deeper than can spring from any human source — rising in his heart, and longs to give it expression not only in his personal but in his public relations.

It is to such men that I address myself on this occasion — to men who believe in an immanent God, and who desire to bring their belief into practice in all their dealings with their fellow men. I am not speaking to men who deny God and Revelation, men who set their mouths against the heavens, and whose tongue walketh through the earth; but to those who are at least willing to believe in a God, and to be guided by Him if His will can be made clear to them. This course of lectures is not delivered in behalf of socialists or political economists, or any of the philosophies of the day; but of a Church which claims to derive its authority from the Word of the Lord, and to believe that that Word, when properly understood, contains a solution of all the problems that affect the welfare of men. The subject is, not the relation of one class of men to another, but of the Church to the State and to secular affairs. It is addressed, therefore, to the members of the Church; or to those who would be members if they could feel satisfied that the Church possesses the truth necessary to meet the wants of the race.

The problem is two-fold : first, Whether the principles of faith and practice that are sufficient to purge the inner life of man, are adequate to correct the evils of the body politic; and second, If they are sufficient, how they are to be applied, whether directly by legislative and collective action, or indirectly through the regeneration of the individual man? Will the religion that saves the citizen save the State; and, if so, how shall it be brought to bear upon the larger body? Must we look outside of the Church for the regeneration of the State; or will the regeneration of the individuals who compose the State answer the purpose? It is not pretended that there is not an important and fundamental function for the State to perform in human concerns, nor that there is no need for reform in the State itself. It is admitted that the State must give effect to spiritual principles before they can serve their full purpose in the emancipation of the race. But the question is, Where shall the process begin, and in what direction shall it operate? Shall it begin at the circumference and work toward the centre, or at the centre and work toward the circumference? Shall the way for the coming down of the kingdom of heaven be prepared by external reforms, or will the coming of the kingdom carry reforms with it? Must all injustice, inequality, and suffering be abolished, and a "diffused happiness" be spread abroad among men, before they will believe in a God, or will a belief in God slowly but surely banish all evil from the earth, and institute a reign of peace and good-will in the world? Is the religion of our Lord and Saviour Jesus Christ adequate to "the healing of the nations," or must it be preceded and supplemented by social reforms, economic measures, and repressive legislation? Is the Word of the Lord strong enough to accomplish the purpose for which it is "sent," or must it return unto Him who sent it "void"? If it is strong enough, by what means shall we bring its interior precepts down into our lowest and most secular affairs?

With regard to the first point, the adequacy of the Word, and of the faith and practice taught in the Word, to meet all the requirements of the human race, we cannot admit a question. This course of lectures is addressed, as has been said, to those who believe in the Word, or who are, at least, willing to believe in it if they can be rationally convinced of its application to all the problems of life. For the purposes of this lecture, therefore, we take the authority of the Word for granted; trusting that what we shall be able to show will strengthen its authority by proving its practical application to all the affairs of our daily life, both private and public.

But the Word is not like any other book. It is divine, not human. Its language is not chosen to express simple human ideas, but to contain the infinite riches of infinite wisdom. It cannot be understood like any other book, and must not be interpreted in the same manner. With regard to the second point, therefore, how the precepts of the Word can be brought down and applied to the manifold relations of secular life, we must appeal to the doctrine of the Church.

Turning, then, to the doctrine of the Church for instruction, we find, in the first place, that the Church does not ignore the existence of secular affairs, or overlook the necessity of taking an active part in them. On the contrary she teaches that man must take such a part; that, if he does not, his religious life will be like a house without a foundation, or a soul without a body; and that it is only in the faithful discharge of our social and secular duties that our religion can find full and adequate expression. In other words, a spiritual life consists, not in shutting ourselves off from the world, nor in spending our time in meditation and prayer apart from active employment, but in bringing spiritual principles to bear in all our outward concerns. The Lord's prayer for the disciples was, not that they should be taken " out of the world," but "kept from the evil." (JOHN xvii. 15.)

This truth is taught particularly in what is said about the relation of spiritual life to moral and civil life. A civil life is a life of conformity to the laws of the State. A moral life is a life according to the moral or ethical principles that a man may entertain. A spiritual life is a life of obedience to the commandments of the Lord. The doctrine of the New Church teaches that, though a man may live a civil and moral life without living a spiritual life, he cannot live a spiritual life without living at the same time a civil and moral life. This is because while a spiritual or religious life has to do primarily with the springs of man's actions — the motives by which he is impelled — it must find expression in a civil and moral life, or it will be dissipated and lost. A spiritual life not resting upon the words and deeds of civil and moral life, will lose consistency and support, and must sooner or later perish. So far then from countenancing the idea that it is the duty of the Church to preach what is called religion, and to let secular affairs severely alone, the doctrines of the New Church teach that it is the duty of the Church to make herself felt on every plane of life, and that without this, our religion is religion only in name, without substance or power.

This is the general statement. But the doctrines of the Church go farther than this. Not only does the Church teach that our spiritual life must find expression in civil and moral affairs, but that this rule applies to all secular duties, not only to our relations with other men as individuals, but as members of the community, the State, and the Church. This is involved in a true understanding of what is meant by the neighbor that is to be loved as ourselves. According to the doctrine of the New Church, the neighbor is not only the individual man or woman with whom we may come in contact, but every larger or smaller society, or combination of men, that may be formed for legitimate purposes. More than this, the doctrine of the Church teaches that a society is the neighbor in a larger and more important sense than any individual. It is composed, not of one, but of many, and the uses it subserves are greater and more far-reaching. The State is a neighbor in a still larger form, not merely because it is composed of a greater number of individuals, but because it extends over them the protection of its laws, affords them facilities for carrying on their employments in safety and with ease, and is as a father to the people. The Church is the neighbor in the largest sense, not only because she includes more people than the State, but because the purpose she subserves is spiritual and eternal, and vital to our spiritual and eternal welfare. Such being the case it follows that we are to be more careful in applying the principles of true religion to the State and to the Church — all organized bodies of men — than in our dealings with individuals. Patriotism is a higher virtue than friendship, and love of the Church greater than love of country; while a sin against the State is of a deeper dye than against any individual belonging to the State.

This truth ought not to need insistence. But it

does. On no other subject is there so much culpable ignorance and moral obliquity as this. Witness the unblushing frauds practised upon banks and other large business organizations, the defalcations among the holders of corporate funds, and the cheating and robbery practised by the officials of the State. Men who would blush to take advantage of an individual, will defraud a great corporation, apparently without the slightest perception of the sin they are committing. They seem to think there is nothing reprehensible in such conduct, except being found out. This is the origin of the common saying that "corporations have no souls;" by which is meant that they have no individual feelings or personal rights that can be injured. Measuring their conduct, not by its inherent character, but by its effect upon others, and not being able to trace its good or ill results upon corporations as upon individuals, men come to the conclusion that the ordinary laws of justice and morality do not apply to corporations. They forget that if corporations have no souls, they themselves have; and that the sin, if any is committed, is committed not against others, but against their own souls. They need to be reminded that any injury done to their fellow men in their corporate capacity, is a greater sin than even a greater injury done to an individual, and will leave a deeper stain upon their character. True religion demands, not only that we should carry out our spiritual principles in all secular affairs, but that we should be more faithful and conscientious in our dealings with larger and smaller combinations of men, than with individuals.

This brings us to the third aspect of the subject — the practical application of the principles of true religion to secular affairs, including our duty to the neighbor, both in an individual and in a corporate capacity. And on this point the teaching of the New Church is clear and unequivocal. We are to bring our highest spiritual aspirations down into act in all our dealings with our fellow men, whether as individuals or as aggregations of individuals, by the same means — by the application of the precepts of the Word, and especially of the Ten Commandments, to practice in the discharge of the duties of our calling; or, in other words, by shunning the evils forbidden in the Decalogue in all our dealings with our fellow men.

I am aware that this may seem to some a lame and impotent conclusion. There is nothing in this doctrine of obedience to the commandments that appeals to the heroic side of human nature. What men are looking for at this age is some "great thing" to do — some great difficulty to overcome or great sacrifice to make — that shall call forth the plaudits of the race. So commonplace and humdrum a remedy for the ills of the times is distasteful, and is seldom or never referred to. Even the pulpit loses sight of the fact that the Ten Commandments were spoken by the

Lord Himself "with a great voice" (EXOD. xx. 1, 19: DEUT. v. 22), that "the people might hear and believe forever" (EXOD. xix. 9); and that, as the Lord's own divinely chosen method of revealing His will to men, they must be adequate for all the needs of the human race. They necessarily include and comprehend the whole duty of man. They constitute the "missing link" between his inner and outer life. They are the Lord's own accommodation of the laws of life to men. They are the means, and the only means, by which the distance between the inmost divine truth, as it exists in the mind of the Lord, and as it is adapted to the minds of men, can be bridged over. When understood in the light of sound doctrine they will be found applicable to all the circumstances of human life, and will correct all the evils to which the race may be exposed.

Of course it is impossible to enter into an exhaustive illustration of this truth in a single discourse. It will be sufficient to say that it is everywhere insisted on in the doctrines of the Church; and that the Ten Commandments themselves are opened and explained in such a manner as to show their applicability to every emergency of life. I cannot refrain, however, from calling attention to one place where the practical nature of the doctrines of the New Church is fully brought out, and the adaptability of the Ten Commandments to all the walks of life fully illustrated. In the little work on "Charity" they are specifically applied to all classes and conditions of men — to priests, or ministers; to magistrates, or the highest officers of the government, whether national, state, or municipal; to the officials under them of every shade and degree; to judges; to commanders of armies, and the officers under them; to common soldiers; to men of business; to workmen; to husbandmen; to commanders of vessels and sailors; and to servants. And with regard to each one the standard is the same. Though the instructions vary with each class according to the nature and importance of the work he performs, one condition is laid down for all men, namely, that they "look to the Lord, shun evils as sins, and sincerely, justly, and faithfully perform the work of their office or calling" (Doctrine of Charity, 101, *et seq.*). To "look to the Lord" is to act from regard to Him in all that we do; to "shun evils as sins" is to refuse to do the evils forbidden in the commandments; and to do this, is to fulfil "sincerely, faithfully, and justly" the duties of our calling. This is all that the Lord requires of us, and all that the welfare and happiness of our fellow men demand. It is to make the civil and moral life which we all ought to live, and which most of us do live, also a spiritual life, by bringing spiritual principles to bear in all our moral and civil conduct. It is to fulfil the law of charity, or love to the neighbor, whether in his individual or corporate capacity.

Here, then, we find the solution of the problem

before us. So far from countenancing that divorce between religion and life sometimes supposed to exist, and so often charged against the Church, it teaches that religion finds its only solid basis and support in the duties of our daily life, and that it must enter into and regulate all our outward conduct both as individuals and as citizens. It teaches that this is to be accomplished, not merely by the establishment of just laws that shall make sins against other men and the State impossible, but by each man in his individual capacity, looking to the Lord, shunning evils as sins, and performing faithfully the duties of his calling. It teaches, in other words, that the Word of the Lord, or the Ten Commandments as an epitome of the Word, are the means, and the only means, by which the distance between the inner and outer life of man can be spanned, and his highest spiritual affections made fruitful in his lowest and most common-place duties. But, inasmuch as obedience to the commandments as such can only be rendered by individual men as the result of repentance toward God and the beginning of a new life from Him, it follows that these principles must be applied by such men acting in their personal capacity, and not by united or legislative action without such a living principle within. The conclusion is that all reforms to be genuine must begin from a religious principle within, and work toward the circumference; must be spiritual and not natural, from the Lord and not from man; and that any reform not acknowledging the Lord in His revealed Word as the Fountain of life and power, though it may possibly serve a temporary purpose in alleviating the wrongs of society in the "transition time" through which we are now passing, must sooner or later fail of its purpose. Let us endeavor briefly to apply this solution of the subject to the problems of the day.

For this purpose let us apply it, in the first place, to the family, as the unit of the State. Let us imagine a family in which every member, so far as his age and understanding will permit, is in the earnest endeavor to look to the Lord, to shun the evils forbidden in the Decalogue as sins against Him, and to fulfil faithfully his part in the common duties. Suppose that each one is in the effort to put away all hatred and anger, all envy and jealousy, all impurity and lust, all desire to take advantage of others or to deprive them of their privileges, and all disposition to misrepresent or even to misunderstand their designs. Suppose that, as is always the case with those who endeavor to shun evils, they find the opposite good affections springing up in their hearts — love of others, a spirit of mutual helpfulness and affection, a tendency to rejoice in each other's welfare, to cover up their faults, to soothe and comfort rather than to annoy and neglect, in short to oil the machinery of the household instead of letting it wear itself out with fret and jar — what would be the result? Would not such a family be a remote image of a heavenly society? Would it not be a model republic? Would it not show forth even in this world the life of the angels in the other? Would it not illustrate the power of the divine truth, when accepted and obeyed in the name of the Lord, to overcome the sinfulness of the human heart, and to inaugurate a reign of "peace on earth, and good will toward men"?

But what is true of the family is true, or may be true, of the community, the state, or the nation. To be sure it requires a loftier flight of the imagination than many of us are capable of, to picture such a condition of things at the present day; but it is not beyond the limits of possibility. Imagine a municipality for instance in which every man, woman, and child, from the highest officer to the humblest citizen, each in his own degree and place, is in the sincere endeavor to shun the evils forbidden in the Commandments in his dealings with the rest. The mayor or chief magistrate of such a government would be a model official. He would be among the people as "one that serveth." Personal ambition, the lust of power and pelf, would be eliminated from his motives. He would seek the greatest benefit of the greatest number in all his actions. He would be continually influenced by "the good of use to the community, and to the individuals in the community." He would be moved, "in common with men that are wise and fear God, to establish useful laws, to see that they are observed, and especially to live under them; and also to appoint intelligent, and at the same time benevolent, officers under him over the people" (Doctrine of Charity, 102). Imagine also that all the officers and citizens were actuated by similar motives; imagine that they were all as faithful and conscientious in their lesser duties as the mayor in his higher office; imagine that they responded to all the efforts of the government in their behalf; imagine that instead of avoiding their just share of the public expenses, they paid their taxes without evasion and with fidelity; imagine that they were as honest in their transactions with the city, as men usually are with individuals, even the street-sweeper being as anxious to do a full day's work as to secure a full day's wages; imagine that they were sincere and upright in all their private dealings with each other, and with the stranger that came within their gates; and what a model city that would be! How would other cities emulate her example! What an influence would she exert upon the business world around her! How would her ports be crowded with shipping, her warehouses with merchandise, and her streets with the cheerful sounds of industry! She would be "the crowning city, whose merchants are princes, whose traffickers are the honorable of the earth" (ISA. xxiii. 8). Such a city would be a paradise to live in, and her citizens among the most prosperous and enviable men of the earth. And all this would be brought about, not by the superior advantages of her situation, not by the greater natural intelligence and industry of her people, nor by the superior acuteness of her lawmakers, but by the application of the Ten Commandments to all private and public affairs.

Let us look at the subject from another point of view. Let us ask ourselves what human intelligence can do, without such a recognition of the Divine Law as I have pictured, to solve the problems of the day.

In the *Forum* for August last, there is a symposium of four articles on "Sentimental Dealing with Crime, and its World-Wide Increase." The first treats of the great strike that had then just closed at Chicago; the second, of anarchism; the third, of the criminal degradation in New York city; and the fourth, of the increase of crime. In not one of them is there recognition of any higher authority than that of society, or the State, nor of any other principles than purely legal or ethical ones. They are all of them a mere balancing of probabilities and possibilities regarding the effect of legislation, education, punishment, and repression of various kinds; nor does any one of them suggest any certain way out of the difficulties in which we are involved. The next number, for September, contains the address of Judge Cooley, as President of the National Bar Association, on "The Lessons of Recent Disorders." The disorders to which he refers are the lynchings of the South, the anarchism of France, and the strikes and boycotts of the North. Here also we notice a total absence of all principles except legal and ethical ones, while the chief object of the paper seems to be to discover whether or not arbitration can be applied with justice and success to controversies between labor and capital.

These articles are not alluded to by way of criticism, but to illustrate the absence of all recognition of Divine authority, in dealing with the burning questions of the day. We see this exhibited in almost all the reform movements of the time. It would seem as if men had lost faith in religion as the conservator of society. Socialists purpose to accomplish the object proposed, not by overcoming the greed and selfishness of the human heart, but by "the abolition of private property in the great material instruments of production." Nationalists, who may be classed as a branch of Socialists, place their chief reliance upon coöperative industries. Single Taxers believe the universal panacea for all the injustice of the time is to be found in placing all taxes on land values. Besides these we have bimetallists and sound-money men, protectionists and free-traders, and every shade and degree of political economists, each of whom firmly believes that the solution of all problems is to be found in his own particular scheme.

This tendency to rely upon human instead of Divine means, is illustrated in the disposition to resort to legislation and organization for every imaginable purpose. No great crime forces itself upon the attention of men, nor does any new method of defrauding society come to light, unless somebody proposes to make it a statutory offence; as if the mere fact of forbidding men to commit certain acts could correct the evil. Witness the lamentable efforts to cure the evils of intemperance by a resort to prohibitory legislation, instead of the moral suasion that was brought to bear with such powerful effect thirty or forty years ago. Witness the proposed plans for the so-called emancipation of women by making her wages the same as man's, in spite of the fundamental laws of value, and giving her a ballot she cannot defend. Witness the innumerable schemes for the establishment of values other than those that grow out of the laws of production and demand; for the regulation of trade by other means than those Divine Providence has instituted in the differences of climate and soil; and for increasing wages and stimulating manufactures by the inflation of the currency.

Where legislation is found too slow and cumbersome, organization is called into play. Societies are formed for all possible and impossible purposes — to suppress vice, to prevent cruelty to animals and to children, to reform dress, to regulate the use of ornaments involving injury to birds and animals, to promote patriotism, to establish good government, to banish the cigarette, and to do almost every other conceivable thing. Nor is this all. Even the sacred work of the Church is invaded and negatived by this spirit. To make up for her lack of vitality and power, the "Institutional Church" is brought into requisition. The gymnasium, the debating society, the literary coterie, and the social meeting, are resorted to to supplement the prayer meeting and the distinctively religious services. All kinds of outward inducements are made use of in order to restrain the evil propensities of men, and to keep their efforts in the right channel.

I do not wish to be understood as condemning these expedients wholesale. I recognize that legislation has an essential part to play in the economy of the human race, and that there are many governmental reforms now agitated to which no effective character can be given except by collective action. I admit with pleasure the necessity and use of organization in order to accomplish general results, and acknowledge with gratitude the great work that has been accomplished by the societies for the prevention of vice, cruelty, etc., and by other movements of a similar nature. I grant freely that much of this kind of work must have been left undone if it had not been for such organizations as I have mentioned, and that in the peculiar period of the world's history in which we are now living they have an important and vital use to perform.

What I protest against is, not the use of such means for the bettering of the race so far as they are proper and beneficial, but the growing tendency to depend upon them instead of the "Thus saith the Lord"; the disposition, which seems to be increasing even in the Church and among the clergy, to put our faith for "the healing of the nations" in humanly-devised prescriptions, instead of the "leaves" of the "Tree of Life"; to trust to our own efforts, instead of the Divine "Arm" that can alone bring salvation to the people. It would seem as if we had arrived at that time of which it is written, "When the Son of Man cometh, shall He find faith on the earth?" and as if for this reason religion had lost all its power over human conduct.

A brief examination will show how utterly futile such remedies are to right the wrongs of the age. At best they can only reach the symptoms of the trouble, while the causes from which they spring remain untouched and still active. A recent writer in an English Review,* has said upon this subject:—

> The State can remove hindrances, the State can minimize temptations of an external kind, the State can improve conditions of life, the State can punish flagrant violations of order, the State can compel mutual interests to be respected by means of taxation, the State can, if inspired by the Church, infuse justice and righteousness into her laws, and into the administration of them. *But she cannot touch the hidden springs of action.* She cannot influence the higher motives of life. She cannot play upon the affections. She cannot enter upon the regions of

---

* Rev. Frederick Relton, in the *Economist*, for October, 1894.

the inner chamber where the soul holds communion with God. Inasmuch as her behests must be carried out by individual men and women, these in the discharge of their duties will be Christian or non-Christian according to their individual relation to God, and not according to their position as members or officials of the State.

All legislation that has for its object the regulation of the outward actions of men (and this is the highest object that legislation can reach), must necessarily be limited to the suppression of crime, and fail to touch the motives from which all crime has its origin. If successful, which it seldom is, it can only punish wrong doing, not eradicate wrong desires. The function of the State is external; that of the Church internal. The State has to do with the outward conduct of men; the Church with their secret motives. The object of the State is, by the enactment of wise laws, to enable the citizen, if he is well disposed, to carry on all just enterprises with safety and dispatch; and, if he is ill disposed, to punish any infraction he may commit upon the rights or property of another. But the State cannot of itself provide either for the cultivation of right motives or the repression of wrong ones. This is the province of the Church, acting under the leadership of the Lord, the great Head of the Church, and in obedience to the Word as His own revelation of His will to men. All reforms not based squarely upon the truths of Revelation, and not growing out of a renewed and regenerated heart on the part of those engaging in them, are superficial; a salve to heal over "slightly" the hurt of the people, and not a sovereign remedy for the fever that is consuming the heart.

But they are not only superficial; they are deceptive. All the crimes that are committed have their source in some form of selfishness or self-love. Nothing can reach and remedy crime, except that which will reach and remedy the selfishness from which it springs. It follows, therefore, that all reforms that are intended to restrain the sins of men, without reaching and changing the motives by which they are actuated, must fall short of their purpose; and that if we could by such means suppress every manifestation of evil, men would be no better at heart than they are now. Nothing but repentance toward God and a new life from Him will make men better; and the more apparently successful the attempt to make them so by any less radical means, the more they will be deceived by it. Even the individual cannot reform himself by such means. He cannot remove evil by his own efforts. The most he can do is to *shun* evil in the name of the Lord and through strength derived from Him, but only the Lord can remove the evil desires from his heart. " Unto God the Lord belong the issues from death." He alone has " the words of eternal life." Any reform not having its origin in Him, and testified to by acts of repentance on the part of the people, is a delusion.

But again, such reforms are not only superficial and deceptive, they are dangerous. If they could be successful they would only serve to defeat the highest purpose of our life in this world, and render all true preparation for the other world impossible. While it is right that evil should be restrained within bounds for the sake of the well disposed, and that for this reason repressive laws should be passed and enforced; it is wrong on the other hand to interfere more than necessary with human freedom. A strong, though perhaps unconscious, tendency of modern reform, is to set things right without individual action; to let coöperation and State interference do the work which it was intended that every man should do for himself; to make the collective man responsible for the individual, instead of the individual for the collective man. The consequence is that we have among us an increasing body of men who believe that society owes them a living, and who act upon the belief; while there are hundreds and thousands who are looking forward to the good time coming when personal responsibility shall be done away with, and the community shall provide for the wants of all alike. This does not seem to be the order of nature. It certainly is not the order of Divine Providence. The Divine law is that every man shall work out his own salvation with fear and trembling, and that for this purpose he shall not be compelled by external laws, but shall compel himself. It is only when he does this that the good he does can be ascribed to him as his own, or the Lord can come in and take away the disposition to do evil. The modern tendency to hedge men about with outward restraints, to protect them against the natural disabilities under which they have been placed, and to provide for their wants by a paternal government, has the unnoticed but deadly effect of weakening their moral stamina and destroying their manhood. It encourages them to hope for some "great expectations" in the future, instead of exerting themselves like men to provide for themselves; to wait in indolence and idleness for society to right their wrongs, instead of setting them right by the use of their own rationality and freedom. We learn from the parable of the talents that men are placed in this world in order that they make the potential powers with which they are endowed their own by using them; that for this purpose the Lord withdraws Himself so far within as never to interfere with human freedom; that He even permits Himself to be regarded as "an hard man" by the indolent and idle, rather than lessen the responsibility of the well disposed; and that no man can refuse to take his full share of responsibility or to hide his talents "in the earth" without doing damage to his own soul.

Finally, we have the example of our Lord and Saviour Jesus Christ in confirmation of this view. Though at the time of His Advent the world was in a far lower moral condition than it is today; though the rich were richer and the poor poorer than in our time; though the vilest slavery then existed that ever stained the annals of history; and though His people were ground down by a despotism more severe than anything we have seen or are likely to see in this age; the Lord Jesus did not attempt to reform outward abuses except by means of the regeneration of individual men. The same writer already quoted says: —

To save the world He would begin by saving the individual men and women who compose it. He dealt with individuals, not with communities. He influenced men directly, not indirectly. He left environment severely and ruthlessly alone. Social questions He did not meddle with, and, when they were brought before Him, He refused to have any thing to do with them. . . . There was no wholesale treatment of human suffering, no dispensing of a universal drug warranted to cure all kinds of diseases. But there was a patient, personal, treatment of individual cases, by methods varying with the character and needs of the patients.

He knew that it was of no use to reform man's environment, without first reforming the man himself; and that if the man were reformed the new life would quickly modify its environment. He knew that if the soul of man did not obtain the heavenly outlook which a belief in immortality alone can give, it would inevitably lay up for itself treasure upon earth. He knew, and He taught, that there are varying degrees of value to the different parts of man's complex nature (none being without its value), and that if a man learned to value rightly his spiritual nature, he would soon assess the comparative worth of all else in him and about him. There were things whose quest was the object of the nations. He did not say that they were evil or unimportant, but that they were not primary. It is not necessary that a man should live. It is necessary that he should be a true man even at the cost of earthly existence.

The Lord Jehovah did not come into the world to save His people from their discomforts, nor even from their crimes, but from their "sins"; not to remodel the outward conditions of society, but to purge and purify its inner life. He did not call upon the nations to put away their "doings," but "the evil of their doings" from before His eyes (ISA. i. 16); and He taught that for this purpose He had redeemed them from the power of their secret or spiritual enemies. He came, the Apostle says, to "destroy the works of the devil" (1 JOHN iii. 8), not to punish the poor, weak, and helpless victims of the devil's power. He delegated to the Church, acting in His name and strength, the power over the spiritual enemies of the human race that He had won by combats with them and victories over them; and if men would reform the world and make it the heaven it was intended to be, they must avail themselves of this power, by looking to Him and shunning evils as sins against Him.

Look unto me, and be ye saved, all the ends of the earth; for I am God, and there is none else. (ISA. xlv. 22.)

Come unto me, all ye that labor and are heavy laden, and I will give you rest. Take my yoke upon you, and learn of me; for I am meek and lowly of heart; and ye shall find rest unto your souls. For my yoke is easy, and my burden is light. (MATT. xii. 28-30.)

Does any one ask me, then, how he can best show forth the religion he professes in his relation to the State and to all secular affairs? I answer, by being a true Christian — by looking to the Lord Jesus Christ, the Redeemer and Saviour of the race, and shunning the evils forbidden in the Decalogue in all his dealings with his fellow men. As a member of the Church, he must be earnest and consistent, always endeavoring to bring spiritual principles to bear even in secular affairs. As a citizen, he must be watchful and faithful, seeking to discharge all his obligations to the State, as to the neighbor in a larger form, and bringing the same fidelity to bear that he makes use of in his relations to individuals. As an official, he must "look to the Lord, shun evils as sins, and discharge faithfully the duties of his position." As a man of affairs, he must be "faithful in business, fervent in spirit, serving the Lord." As an employer, he must endeavor to do full justice to his employees, and to promote their welfare by every means in his power. As an employee, he must strive to render a full equivalent for all that he receives. His first aim must be to fulfil the law of charity, and only secondarily to supply his own wants. He must not be unmindful of the sufferings of his fellow men. He must do all that lies in his power to discourage evil and to encourage virtue. He must not neglect such outward reforms as seem to him wise and effective, but must bring the highest spiritual truth to bear in so doing.

He must be, in short, a zealous and high-minded member of the Church, a conscientious and upright citizen of the State, a kind neighbor and faithful friend, an affectionate husband and father — a broad-minded, liberal-hearted, noble man. His Christianity must not be confined to his own salvation, but must reach out toward his fellow men of every degree. In this way he will find an adequate outlet for his spiritual affections. The new life that has taken possession of his soul will flow down and animate all his words and deeds. His love toward the Lord within will express itself in love to the neighbor without — not in mere sentiment and kind wishes, but in the faithful discharge of every duty. He will be a "four-square" man. Every side of his character will be fully developed. He will be animated by the purest affections, guided by the highest truth, and live the most disinterested life. His will be the "full measure of a man, that is, of an angel."

The conclusion is, that what the world needs today is the full and complete marriage of religion and life. All the disadvantages under which we are laboring can be traced to the decay of vital and practical religion, and nothing less than the reestablishment of such religion can remove them. Capital punishment, though it may have been right and proper in the past, has never been able to do away with murder, and never will. Nothing but repentance of that hatred which is the essence of murder, and which, as well as the outward act, is forbidden in the Ten Commandments, can do that. The most severe laws against theft and embezzlement have never succeeded in making men honest; only that integrity of heart that is inculcated in the highest sense of the Commandment, "Thou shalt not steal," can have that effect. The penalties against perjury cannot make men truthful; only that perfect sincerity that renders men as open as the day, can bring about such a result. The legislation which is now being resorted to more than ever before to make men pure, can at best only find out and punish a chance victim of the dreadful evil, while the lust from which it springs will be as strong as ever. On the other hand, what a revolution would be wrought in society if a pure and undefiled religion could be carried out among men! Suppose, for instance, that the officials of one of our large and corrupt municipalities could be brought in a single night to genuine and intelligent repentance; suppose they could even be made sincerely and transparently truthful; what a radical and beneficent change it would work in the administration of the government, without the repeal of a single ordinance or the dismissal of a single officer, and how thoroughly would all rascality and double-dealing disappear from the political horizon! There is more power in a single one of the Ten Commandments, when intelligently understood and thoroughly applied, than in all the ethics or philosophies that were ever invented by men. What the world needs, therefore, is not so much wiser laws, as a disposition to interpret correctly and apply faithfully the laws that already exist; not so much reform, as religion; not so much repression and regulation, as repentance and regeneration; not so much what is blindly called "the mind of Christ," as simple obedience to the Ten Commandments in which His mind is clearly revealed; and until men begin to realize this truth, all the hue and cry so popular at the present day after a new economy and social progress, will be found a snare and delusion. Not until men hear the bugle call of the Church, accept the "Thus saith the Lord" as the only safe rule of life, and do the work of repentance daily, can they expect any full or final relief from the evils they have brought upon themselves by their neglect of these things.

To the law and to the testimony; if they speak not according to this word, it is because there is no light in them. (ISA. viii. 20.)

PAUPERISM AND CRIME

Theodore F. Wright

THE POOR.

When our Lord said to those who at the supper in Bethany objected to the use of the ointment by Mary, that they had the poor always with them, He used a term, *ptochoi*, which was of old the word for beggars. Derived from a root meaning crouching or cringing, it was found appropriate to designate the class of people who crouched by the waysides in Greece and Palestine beseeching alms by rattling their cups or stretching out deformed hands. The money might have been given to the poor, they said, scattered among the beggars on the morrow. This is declared to have been the suggestion of Judas, not that he cared for the poor, but that he cared for the money.

If there were not ample evidence that the Holy Land abounded in beggars, the use of this word and the saying that the poor were always with them would testify that abject poverty was to be seen everywhere.

The widow's mite tells a tale of misery meagrely relieved by dole, which needs no comment.

From that day to this the poor have been always with us. Much has been done for them. Great crimes have sought for expiation in hospitals and refuges erected for them by the rich and powerful. But the cringing and crouching are still with us. It is however the spirit of the present day to deal with fundamental problems rather than with surface indications; to seek to remove the causes of such misery rather than merely to relieve existing distress; and those who would be neighbors to the suffering must do more than pour oil and wine into the wounds and bear to a place of healing, they must even seek that no more may fall by that way of past peril.

The problem of the poor as it presents itself to-day is not, What shall be done to carry them through this winter or the next? It is not, What is the best way of diminishing the public expense on account of the pauper element? It is rather, What is the cause of this state of things? and what is its remedy? A deplorable condition extending from the remote past to the present, demands of us no mere palliative, although that part of the treatment is imperatively necessary to be applied now and for a long time to come; but it demands a cure, a gospel of deliverance.

Thoughtful people divide at this point on all such questions. There are those who have little hope of the future, and who regard as dreams all theories of ultimate cure of evil, who are content with slight improvements upon the manifestly unsuccessful treatment of public evils in the past, and who deprecate as Quixotic all talk of effective remedies.

But there is another party consisting of those who feel the spirit of a new and final age, to which the glorious promises of the Scriptures shall ultimately be applicable, and these cannot work for the day alone but must reach backward into history and downward into existing conditions and onward into a hopeful future. To such the faith of the New Church comes as an interpreter of their visions and an instructor of their efforts, tempering enthusiasm with patience, and at the same time giving vast encouragement to zealous labors. "Behold, I make all things new," is the watchword of today's battle with old evils.

THE DIVINE PROVIDENCE UNIVERSAL.

Before entering with some hope upon this broad subject I must postulate the Divine Love and Wisdom of the Creator. If obliged to take the ground that the Divine Providence is a limited and irregular care of the world, one might be forced to conclude the really atheistic doctrine that men have been created to strangle each other until the mightiest prosper and obtain the lion's share of this world's goods, even as a pack of wolves contest for their prey. It would then follow that the present condition is an orderly stage in human development; that Malthus was right in predicting overpopulation as the inevitable result, and destructions by war and pestilence and famine as the only remedy; and that the future will be like the past, only more and more full of frantic struggle, until the Napoleonic few shall possess the world, clothed in purple and fine linen and faring sumptuously every day, while the beggar at the gate has disappeared, having been trampled to death by the feet of the rich neighbors who came to the repasts of which the rule was that only they were to be bidden who could return the invitation.

This state of things, though easily conceivable, will never be. If the struggle for life were, as some suppose, the only mode of progress, such an end might be expected; but "the earth is the Lord's and the fulness thereof, the world and they that dwell therein." An infinite love has given birth to it, an infinite wisdom has formed it, and an infinite design is in everything that is made. There was some perception of this grand unity among the ancients, but only in the unfolding of the truth of Scripture through the instrumentality of Swedenborg has the doctrine been fully and clearly enunciated that every human soul has its place in the UNIVERSAL MAN, and that, when souls become obedient to the Divine leading, a plan, formed before the foundation of the world, is carried out, and a countless multitude of the redeemed dwell with their Creator as the bride of the Lamb.

In this aspect of the case we see that there is room enough and air enough and bread enough for all, and that it could be only by some interference with the Divine plan that pauperism could arise. In the exercise of mental aptitudes for industry, as provided by the Father of all, and in the interchange of the products of their labor, all would be provided for. None would be idle and none would seriously suffer, but a universal interdependence would support all, as the members of the physical body are supported.

The Bible gives us some glimpses of this when it shows us how, by the natural increase of his flocks, Abraham became rich without depriving any other of what was rightfully his, and without in any way preventing all others from receiving the same benefits. The little country of Palestine was never comparable with many others in respect to its productiveness, but it would be easy to show that there need never have been abject poverty in it. When the Israelites entered upon it, each family was provided with land and with an opportunity to secure the comforts of life, and we see in a general way the working of this Divine plan of national thrift.

Allowing somewhat for poetic fervor, we see the same condition described as follows by Hesiod when speaking of the Golden Age : —

All blessings were theirs; of its own will, the fruitful field bare them fruit, much and ample; they gladly reaped the labors of their hands in quietness, being rich in flocks. Nor was wretched old age impending, but they died as if overcome by sleep.

HOW POVERTY AROSE.

What brought this happy and prosperous condition to an end? Again the Scripture makes ready answer. Samuel, the last of the Judges, was asked by the people to make them a king. He was grieved, for he saw what would follow, and he took their wish to the Lord and brought back the answer: —

> This will be the manner of the king that shall reign over you: He will take your sons and appoint them for himself, for his chariots and his horsemen. And he will set them to plough his ground and reap his harvest and make his instruments of war. And he will take your fields and your vineyards and your oliveyards, the best of them, and give to his officers. And he will take your menservants and your maidservants and your goodliest young men and your asses, and put them to his work. And ye shall be his servants. And ye shall cry out in that day because of your king which ye have chosen.
>
> Nevertheless the people said, Nay, but we will have a king over us, that we also may be like all the nations, and that our king may judge us, and go out before us, and fight our battles. (1 SAM. viii. 10–20.)

It will be seen that Israel craved a king in order to be on an equality with other nations as regards war. Egypt and other countries were in the hands of mighty rulers who kept standing armies, and Israel felt that it must appeal to the same resource.

The result was manifest elsewhere and justified the ominous words of Samuel. The king impoverished his people by taking whatever his campaigns required. In successful warfare the booty was chiefly his. In order to feed his forces he must not only levy taxes, but must also have large domains of his own. His domain, chosen from the best of the land, would of course bear no taxation. The longer this state of things lasted, the larger would be the possessions of the king, and by inevitable consequence the smaller would be the possessions of the people. Theoretically perhaps the king should have no private fortune; practically he always had an enormous and constantly increasing private fortune.

One cause of this perversion of the Divine plan with all its attendant evils seems to have been war. There was war before this, to be sure, for the Israelites were to drive out their enemies as they advanced; but their struggles hitherto had not been severe, nor costly, nor long continued. No standing army had been necessary to do the will of God when the robber tribes invaded their fields. It was because they were losing their faith in God and substituting for it a reliance upon earthly resources, that they felt compelled to have a king. They did not rebuke Samuel as an untruthful prophet. They admitted the truth of his prediction, while they declared that still they would have a king. It was a degenerate day compared with that of Joshua, and Israel was blindly copying the ways of sinful peoples. Only evil could follow. Only evil did follow. The moderate but general prosperity of the people gave way to luxury and the beggar.

War will never be painted blacker than it is. As it became the trade of the Middle Ages, agriculture, the only source of general comfort, was despised in comparison with the military life which consumed everything and produced nothing, until the barons became the only landowners. There is in our day a certain activity of industry produced by war because armies must be fed and clothed and paid, but the ultimate increase of burden is inevitable, while the soil loses those that should till it. "Bread and games" was the remedy in Rome for popular unrest, but these were no remedy; pensions and public kitchens are talked of now, but again we have no remedy.

EXISTING PAUPERISM.

It may be well to stop for a brief survey of the existing pauperism, the utter hopelessness of many, which has gradually been developed. In England, according to the statistics collected by Mulhall, there are three paupers in every one hundred of the population, in Scotland and Ireland nearly as many. The number of paupers in the city of London is set down at the enormous number of one hundred and two thousand, and their cost is something like one million pounds sterling per annum. In the United Kingdom the cost of providing for the poor who are at public charge, has increased from eight million pounds per annum in 1850 to eleven million pounds in 1889. Bramwell Booth's report of Salvation Army work for 1894 says that there are one hundred thousand paupers in London, thirty thousand abandoned women, thirty-three thousand homeless adults, thirty-five thousand slum children; ten thousand new criminals added yearly. "The most utterly hopeless specimen of man yet discovered or evolved is the constant hearer of goody-goody addresses and the habitual recipient of hot victuals for which he does nothing but lie."

But figures seem less instructive than individual cases. Let me therefore bring to view a few such, taken from a calm book, "Pauperism and the Endowment of Old Age," by Charles Booth, an Englishman, but not of the Salvation Army family. Here is the case of a man named Martin whose wife is named Eliza. The man has been a dock laborer. He was admitted to Bromley workhouse because of failing sight. His wife was already in the hospital, having broken a leg while intoxicated. When she came out of the hospital she was admitted to the workhouse. Both are drunkards. She sometimes goes out, but soon returns, always in bad condition. They had three children, Patrick, James, and Bridget. Patrick has been twice in prison for theft. He has been fifteen years in the marines, but was discharged for the good of the service. He has been in and out of the workhouse several times, and is now likely to finish his days there, though but forty years old. James is a laborer, who has married and then deserted his wife and is living with another woman. Bridget married and bore four children. Her husband deserted her, was sent to prison for it, and then returned to her, but she deserted him and is living with another man. Then her husband went to the workhouse with the children. All the connections of this family are paupers or thieves or otherwise immoral. And the children follow the parents.

Another case: The man was sent to prison for two years for assault. Then his wife was admitted to the workhouse. He came there later. After spending the winter he went out in August to pick hops. After the season he returned, and has done this for several years. His wife has died. Again: a man who had spent all his money at public houses was brought in sick. His father had been admitted after doing no work for five years. His aunt and uncle were in the workhouse. So was his sister. Another case described is that of a widow who could get no work, who came into the workhouse for most of the year eight times and at last to remain.

Details are given by Mr. Booth of more than sixty cases, and in every case it appears that no sudden misfortune brought the subject to public charge, but that it was a combination of circumstances from which no successful effort was made to escape. On this point I again cite this author, for he has carefully analyzed the cases in three large workhouses. In St. Pancras the percentage of those who are there because of drink is twenty-two, old age twenty-three, sickness twenty-one, while laziness is credited with ten per cent. It is noticeable that all these people have an occupation, women as well as men, and that nine out of ten seem willing to work when they can get work.

As to the causes of pauperism, Mr. Booth says: —

> It is easy to exaggerate any one of them at the expense of the rest. Incapacity and mental disease might be stretched to cover almost all. Vice, drink, and laziness, themselves closely bound together, fill also a great place in connection with sickness and lack of work — or we may reverse this, and show how sickness and lack of work, and the consequent loss of proper food, end in demoralization of all kinds, and especially in drink. It is said also that the chief cause of pauperism is to be found in our attempts to relieve it.

CRIME.

With this closing remark I do not deal because at this point it seems necessary to point out that this pauperism is very closely connected with crime. Crime appears in almost all the specific cases described. It is perhaps unnecessary to go into details. Thieving, assaults, and crimes against chastity seem to be the accompaniments of this pauper life in most cases. Behind the poverty is some wickedness which has defeated all attempts at reform. With the basest heredity these people seem to have only the animal nature developed, and self-control under temptation is unknown.

There are of course many crimes — murder, adultery, forgery, and embezzlement — which either do not belong to one grade in society more than to another, or are possible only to positions of trust; but apparently these poor creatures whom we are now considering are born, live, and die in an atmosphere of crime, commit more or less crime during their active years, and bring up at last in the workhouse because of damaged bodies worn out by excesses.

WAGE-EARNERS' DISCONTENT.

Beginning at this lowest level of humanity in our communities, we may rise somewhat without getting out of the range of actual need and grinding poverty. The laborer who finds work for only a part of the year, yet has his rent to pay for twelve months; the mill-hand, whose wages are barely sufficient in good times, but who suffers reduction of wages or total cessation of them when the market is depressed; the mechanic, whose habits in early life make no provision for the future; and the women working on clothes and the like for the merest subsistence — all these and others are in danger of becoming public charges. He who lays nothing by in his active manhood, whether the cause is extravagance or misfortune, is sure, I assume, to be in debt ere long and in the end to be a burden upon others. He knows this, but he hopes that in some way times will change or the conditions of thrift be relaxed, so that he may avoid the end which old age generally witnesses.

And it is these classes rather than the paupers, who are so full of discontent and so easily roused to rebellion as to threaten very seriously the permanence of our institutions. They believe that certain evils may be remedied by legislation and they clamor for such laws as they desire. Wholly unaware of the impossibility of mere legislative remedies except to cure manifest injustice, they lean in the main on a broken reed, and their agitations only disturb trade without benefit to any one. The strike may do in prosperous times, though then it is seldom called for, but to resort to it in times of financial distress is an appalling blunder often repeated and with increasing irritation on the part of the unsuccessful. It has been found that an appeal to violence by strikers is sure to be put down with force, and the loss of life and property is a sad concomitant which will be avoided in any well-regulated country.

CAPITALISM.

It must be confessed here in passing that the capitalist sometimes needs correction rather than his operatives, and it is impossible to excuse Mr. Pullman and his enormously lucrative methods of business, when it is clear from the testimony recently taken that he rents his tenements to workmen at a price representing a valuation of nine hundred dollars for each room; that an employee received in the year $345.68, was charged $15.71 a month for rent and water, and so had but $157.16 or forty-three cents a day left whereon to feed and clothe his wife, two children, and himself; and that the boasted giving of men work during dull times was just to the extent of getting their rents paid.* Still I should say that neither legislation nor strikes would help the workmen at Pullman, and that, in seeking aid from either, they only showed how easily they could be misled by bad counsels. These people always have the sympathy of the country until they use violence, and then they are declared to be public enemies.

PENSIONS FOR OLD AGE.

The remedy proposed by Mr. Booth for the pauperism which he has minutely described in the volume above cited, is pensions payable to old age. He finds that these people marry young and spend their wages improvidently. He would therefore tax them in early life, and repay these taxes to them in old age. There are several such schemes in England, but their de-

---

* See *Bibliotheca Sacra*, January, 1895, p. 184.

tails are unimportant to us because they are obviously only palliatives. Indeed they might promote pauperism by taking away even what inducement to save now exists. The tax would be paid very unwillingly, as the young man would claim that he needed his money, and he would the more readily cast himself on the town in the belief that it had defrauded him. Then the old paupers, feeling that they had provided for themselves, would be less likely to do anything but lie about. This pension looks like a premium on pauperism. Moreover, who intends at twenty to be a pauper at seventy, and so is ready to be levied on for a tax?

PRINCIPLES WANTED.

The difficulty with this and all similar schemes is that they proceed from no principle. They simply find a condition, and they say, "How can this be mollified?" They deal with humanity in a hopeless spirit. It is "bread and games" again, as at Rome.

Let me enumerate a few principles which must be reckoned with, or we shall do more harm than good by our attempted charity, and I would state them in the words of our teachings:—

Charity is believed to consist in giving to the poor, but it consists in the promotion of good. He who gives aid to a villain does evil to his neighbor through him. Charity consists in doing right in every calling. To do injustice is to hate the neighbor. Every man is our neighbor, but distinctly; a society more than one person, the country still more, the Lord's kingdom still more, the Lord most of all. (Arcana Cœlestia, 8120–8123.)

And note the following from the "True Christian Religion":—

The love of self wishes well to no one, nor to the country, except for the sake of self. It does good for its own sake alone. In the love of self one loves others only as his slaves. (n. 396.)

Man is not born for his own sake, but for the sake of others. (n. 406.)

A man is to be loved according to the quality of the good in him. (n. 409.)

To love the neighbor as one's self is not to despise him, but to deal justly with him. (n. 411.)

He who loves society loves those of whom society consists. In doing good to society he consults for the good of each individual. (n. 412.)

The country is to be loved more than self. (n. 414.)

Love for the Lord's kingdom is love to the neighbor in its fulness. (n. 416.)

To be useful is to do good. (n. 419.)

True charity is to do good continually in the employment in which a man is engaged. He works daily, and when he is not at work, the thought of it is in his mind. Thus he becomes more and more charity in form. Such do not place merit in works, because they do not think of that but of their duty. (n. 423.)

There are duties prescribed by statute law, by common law, and by moral law. They who are in charity perform all these justly and faithfully. (n. 432.)

The first part of charity is to remove evil, the second to do good. So far as one does not desire evil, he desires good. No man can purify himself by his own strength, yet the power given him by the Lord seems to be his own. The Lord gives this appearance to every man for the sake of his salvation. (n. 438.)

The commandments given at Sinai are in all kingdoms of the world, and were in Egypt from which the Israelites had come, and they were the law of civil justice, without which no kingdom could exist; but they were written by God on stone because they are the precepts also of spiritual life. Transfer the external moral life prevailing in society into the internal man, so that the will and thought are like the act, and you will have true charity. (n. 445.)

God loves every man, yet He can do good to him only through other men. (n. 457.)

Also these:—

If charity were first and faith second in the church, the church would be different. The church would then be one, containing all who are in a good life, both within Christendom and outside of it. (Arcana Cœlestia, 6269.)

In heaven there are innumerable societies, all distinct, yet constituting one heaven, because all are in the love of the Lord and the neighbor. (*Ibid.* 2982.)

Man can shun evils as of himself by the power given him by the Lord, if he implores it. (Doctrine of Life, 31.)

So long as man does not shun evils as sins, the evils close the inner mind and prevent it from being opened. (*Ibid.* 86.)

The Divine Providence is universal. (Arcana Cœlestia, 2694.)

It is not only with the good, but with the evil. (Divine Providence, 287.)

Divine Providence with the evil is a continual permission of evil in order that there may be withdrawal from it. (*Ibid.* 296.)

No one is predestined to hell. The purpose of creation is a heaven from the human race. Every man is created that he may come into heaven. Every man can be saved, and they are saved who ackowledge God and live uprightly. It is man's fault if he be not saved. (*Ibid.* 322.)

The balance of all things in the other life is such that evil punishes itself. (Arcana Cœlestia, 696.)

The punishment of retaliation comes from this law of heavenly order, "All things whatsoever ye would that men should do to you, do ye even so to them." They who do good from the heart receive good from others, and they who do evil, receive evil. To every good its reward is joined, and to every evil its punishment. (*Ibid.* 8214.)

APPLICATION.

In the light of these principles we see at once that there is a government in the world, namely, that of the good Providence of the Lord, who is no respecter of persons, and that any course pursued in our dealings with our fellow men which cooperates with this Divine Law, will be just in itself and will be in the line of ultimate success. These teachings rebuke many things, such as indiscriminate almsgiving, contempt for any one, thought of any one as hopelessly bad, neglect to punish crime, disregard of the rights of any race or condition, efforts to secure temporary peace at the cost of any injustice, doing evil in recklessness to obtain wealth or comfort or place, and especially indulging any hatred towards those who may be ignorant or shiftless or depraved. Success in wealth-getting is no success at all, unless the qualities of a true manhood be developed. An avaricious greed is no better than an improvident wastefulness. There is a just punishment for every wrong, and it should be impartially administered. At the same time the love of the sinner, but not of his sin, should lead all right-minded people to put themselves into the Lord's hands as servants of His in leading men away from evil and into an abhorrence of it, which is the necessary preliminary to their loving good and being good. As the Lord deals with individuals, so must we come into personal relations with the erring for their souls' sake.

CONFIRMATIONS.

That these principles are right, all experience testifies. Given to the world a century ago in a manner so quiet as to leave every one in perfect freedom to receive or reject them, they have found their way unconsciously into the minds of many laborers in the cause of fallen man, until "not alms, but a friend" has become the motto of work for the needy, until great care is exercised to give no aid to wrong, and until there is a general wisdom manifested in all the relations of benefactor and beneficiary which will certainly never be abandoned in favor of the older, less rational, and less kindly methods, and which deserves and will have success, for the Lord is on its side.

It is also a cause for rejoicing that in legislation there is a growing regard for the rights of all, less favoring of great monopolies than formerly, and a tendency to place all on an equal footing.

The late humiliating example of the Senate of the United States apparently controlled by a few unscrupulous men for the sake of their own gain as against the welfare of the country, has received such general condemnation that evidence is given of the gradual development of a public conscience which regards the poor as well as the rich. How far the prevalent suspiciousness of the poor towards the rich, which is seen in various ways, is justified, it is difficult to say, but it cannot be denied that great wealth has sometimes come to the speculator who does nobody any good, while the hard-working agriculturist has seemed to be deprived of his fair reward. I must be allowed to express the hope that the time may come when, after the lottery business has been put down by the force of law and public sentiment, stock-gambling may also receive its doom.

CLASSIFICATION.

As to what shall be done with the pauper, it is evident that careful classification must be made. The unfortunate must not be confounded with the unworthy. There is something wrong in the system described in the English work referred to, when people able to work idle away the winter at the public expense, and then go out for a season's profligacy only to return more wicked and shiftless than before. Already in this country we know better than that. Such people would be put under sentence, and would be compelled to work for a sufficient time to make some change in them, and then they would be watched as probationers.

When we have really classified the paupers, we shall know much better what to do. The aged, whose continued feebleness has exhausted their resources, will be tenderly and thoroughly cared for in places worthy of them and of the community providing for them. Such places will not be almshouses but homes. If we put a soldier into a home because he has spent his strength for the country, so ought we to do with all faithful workers who may come at last, through no serious fault of their own, to need a refuge wherein they may receive the hospitality of the town.

On the other hand, there are classes to whom we are too indulgent, and so increase the evil. The tramp — we laugh at him for his folly and are satisfied if he moves on. We should have the eyes to see that thereby we are developing a criminal class of the worst type, drunken, thieving, and murderous. Instead of this joking and this feeding of these idlers, we should catch every one of them, should regard it as an offence against law to have no occupation, and should set them to work making roads until they come to themselves. It would be expensive and laborious at first, but the fact is that sooner or later it must be done, for the evil will grow until it will imperatively demand that the obvious remedy be applied. If it be not already settled in law, let it be settled at an early day, that the State demands the work of every citizen and will enforce its demand upon every vagrant.

Our prisons would not be so full if we had proper workhouses and if we filled them. Nor would our insane asylums overflow if it were not for this great crime of idleness so prevalent with the tramp and with the street girl and with the saloon loafer. Work is their only avenue of reform, as it is with us all. The State must pursue them until they either find work or receive it under duress. In all this, however, the agents must be humane while firm and persistent.

THE PROPER AGENTS.

Even in what we have done in this respect we have as a rule employed the wrong people as our agents, because they themselves were without principle, profane and drunken; and thus there was no contact of the misguided with those in whose ways they could see something to emulate. Formerly we cared too little who were teachers of the young, but now we do care. We shall come in time to care just as much who are the mentors of our criminals, and then a better day will be near, with less of brute force and actual cruelty in discipline, and more of intelligence and of the spirit of the shepherd with the sheep that are gone astray.

MORAL AGENCIES.

As to the restless work-people in the mills and on the railways, the same principle holds — firm friendship. Men used to know their employer, and he knew them. Now he does not know them, perhaps he keeps away from them, and perhaps he hates them. But a great company of working-people can no more be managed by a man for whom they have no respect than an army can be. It is folly to think that the human element of mutual regard can be eliminated, while still coöperation remains. In some way the corporations and especially the managers must come into friendship for and with their employees, and the longer they postpone this effort, the more strikes and recrimination we shall have. But we have only to turn to those employers who do not suffer from strikes, to see that they recognize in some way the fact of mutual dependence and treat their people with justice, as men and women, and not as mere "hands."

Tolstoi has pointed out that the folly of the poor of Moscow is due to their imitation of the rich, and he has also declared that the rich care so little for the poor that they will turn their power to no good account. There is truth in this. In this country the rich are often boastful in word and manner and dress and equipage and house, and this leads to extravagance in the poor in their effort to be as much "in style." It is to be hoped that this vulgarity of wealth will some time learn to value character above display, and then we shall not see hard-earned money squandered in ways which only temporarily satisfy false and foolish ambitions. When the rich say nothing about their wealth and cease to be anxious to display it, one great cause of poverty will be removed at once. Less jewelry will then be bought, and more bread. We shall have less gaudiness and more goodness.

RESPECT FOR USE.

Since the Lord has given us all the power to be useful in some distinct way, and since our highest possible achievement is to perform this use, therefore we must respect usefulness with a genuine regard. Wealth, fame, popular control, and all like matters must not be our aim, nor the object of our heartiest commendation, but rather we must show in all our dealing with others that our highest regard goes out to the industrious, and the faithful, and the helpful. We should not undervalue the recreations of life, but we should value most its activities. With so healthful a sentiment as this in the community, juster ideas of honorable toil would prevail, and we should avoid much of the extravagance of youth inevitably leading to pauperism in the end. Moreover people would prefer a moderate compensation for a work clearly useful, to a high salary for doing no good; and discontent upon the farm, now working great mischief, would diminish.

It is this exaltation of the real above the seeming, of the permanent above the temporal, of the spiritual above the natural, which it is the especial object of the teachings of the New Church to inculcate, and I cannot better close this imperfect presentation of them than by quoting a few words from a passage in the "Arcana," wherein we read: —

To be the least in heaven is to be the greatest, and to be humble is to be high, and to be poor and needy is to be rich and well endowed. They who are in external thought alone cannot understand this, for they think that the least can never be greatest, nor the humble high, nor the poor rich. Still so it is in heaven; but they do not know it, and so long as they are in externals only, they are neither willing nor able to know it. In heaven he who knows, confesses, and in heart believes that no power is from self, but all from the Lord, is called the least, yet he is the greatest, for he has power from the Lord. So it is with him who is humble; for, confessing that he has no intelligence and wisdom of himself, he is endowed by the Lord with power, intelligence, and wisdom more than others. Again, he is called poor and needy who believes in his heart that he possesses nothing of his own; he is rich and well endowed in heaven, for the Lord gives him all riches, and he is wiser and more wealthy than others and lives in magnificence and in the midst of treasure. (n. 4459.)

CONCLUSION.

The summing up of these thoughts is, that the good Lord has made every one to fill a distinct place; that many are not in such usefulness nor on the way to it because of adverse conditions arising in war and otherwise; that nevertheless it is the duty of the right-minded not to excuse or by neglect to increase such disorders, but to apply to their remedy the immutable principles which lie at the foundation of Divine order, and that in so doing careful classification is the necessary preliminary to be followed by just and steadfast discipline; and that there is much in present social custom which tends to perpetuate hard feeling and improvidence, and that here the wrong-doers should be at once rebuked. Moreover, it is urged that we must all work on this great task, as individuals with an interest in individuals, and that we must do this as a part of our religion, that is, of our neighborly love.

In this union of churches for this work of uplifting the unmoral and immoral classes, there is the true bond of brotherhood in the Lord Jesus. It is vastly more profound and every way permanent than any mere external combination. As the prophet saith:—

They helped every one his neighbor; and every one said to his brother, Be of good courage; and the Lord said, I have chosen thee, and not cast thee away. (ISA. xli. 6, 9.)

NATURAL AND SPIRITUAL HEALTH

JAMES REED

It was stated in the introductory chapter that the doctrines of the New Church, as understood by those who accept them, are a complete system of spiritual laws. They do not merely define in a new and different manner certain points of theology, but throw fresh light on all subjects of human thought. They teach not only a new faith, but a new philosophy. Thus doing, they present Christian belief, life, and worship on grounds which are philosophical and rational. We are not required to take on trust Divine and spiritual mysteries which are above our comprehension; but the truth comes to us as something that appeals to our reason and judgment and finds its support in the undoubted facts of nature and science. The system is not only comprehensive, but connected throughout. It not only takes into account the vital points of religious belief, but shows them in their relation to each other, and to all truth. It is no exaggeration to say that, when they are received, they seem as clearly evident and demonstrable as the law of gravitation, or any undisputed principle of physical science. Thus faith becomes the friend and ally of reason. The real truth concerning God's nature and providence, the Holy Scriptures, the life here and the life hereafter, is seen to be something which man's intellect can comprehend as clearly and explain as rationally as he can comprehend and explain the facts of his earthly history or the phenomena of his natural existence.

The great key to the distinctive philosophy of the New Church is the doctrine, so called, of Discrete Degrees. One cannot but marvel at the flood of light which this doctrine throws on all subjects. Let me endeavor to define it as briefly and concisely as possible.

Our first experience in life is that of finding ourselves in a natural or material world. We did not come here through any will or purpose of our own, but were called into being by a power other than ourselves. We see around us sun, moon and stars, water, earth and clouds, hills and mountains, valleys and plains, animals, plants and stones, in endless variety, together with other objects fashioned by human hands. These visible things are at first the only things of which we have any knowledge. We see about us also human forms, men like ourselves. We see our own bodily forms, and are confronted with the necessity of providing for them food, clothing, and shelter. They must be protected from the sun's excessive heat, from the bitter cold of winter, and from the raging tempest. They must be nourished by the substances which the earth supplies, else they will waste away and perish. This first external view of human conditions makes the natural world appear to be the whole of the created universe. But, after a while, if we are wise, we begin to perceive that it is not the whole; yea, that it is but the least and lowest part of that which God has created. The body which we see is only the outward form and clothing of something which we do not see. Within the body, superior to and exercising control over it, is a power, a human individuality, which loves and thinks, and makes the body do its bidding. A corpse has all the organs and members which a living body possesses; but they are wholly unserviceable. It has eyes, but there is no sight; ears, but there is no hearing. And why? Because that indwelling something which we call soul or spirit, and which used the body for its earthly tabernacle, has departed. Sensation is gone, because the power to take cognizance of anything by means of the senses is gone. The loving, thinking, and reasoning part of the being, who once dwelt in the body, no longer has his home there.

Now let us try to lay hold of this vital truth, namely, that the spirit and the body are wholly distinct from each other. By no possible means can the spirit become matter, or matter be converted into spirit. When brought together in a living person, they act as one; but in reality it is the spirit which acts, the body is only acted upon. The two belong to entirely different planes or degrees of life; in truth, they belong to two different worlds. According to the teachings of the New Church, the spiritual world is an inner world, bearing the same relation to the soul or spirit of man that the world of nature bears to his body. By no possibility can it be seen with natural eyes or touched with natural hands. We do not see the souls or spirits of our friends while they are living in the flesh; we are made conscious of their presence only by means of the bodies which they inhabit; and yet we know perfectly well that they themselves are not those bodies. What we love is not their physical forms and features, but the higher spiritual nature to which the forms and features give expression. When, however, the body dies, the spirit wakes to consciousness in the world to which it belongs, and of which it forms a part. It sees with its own spiritual eyes, hears with its spiritual ears, and touches with its spiritual hands — in a word, it is clothed with a spiritual body. This is according to the apostle's teaching: "There is a natural body, and there is a spiritual body." The world in which it finds itself is real and substantial, full of visible objects ready for its use, full of human beings clothed with spiritual bodies like its own. Even so near is that other world to this. But no line of demarcation could be clearer and sharper than that which exists between the natural and the spiritual part of a human being. It is the distinction of Discrete Degrees. The relation between the two is not that of continuity, but of correspondence. That is to say, the two act and react on each other. The one is to the inner world what the other is to the outer world; but neither can cross the line by which they are divided.

Not only are the soul and body of man distinct from each other and yet united by correspondence, but all the operations of the mind through the body stand in a similar relationship. We listen to the voice of a speaker; what we hear is words. Vibrations made by him on the air affect our ears with the sensation which is called sound. These words, or sounds, are purely natural or physical effects; but they are the recognized mediums of something which is far more than physical. They convey to us, from him who utters them, the thoughts of his mind. Those thoughts, as they exist unexpressed in his mind, could not possibly be apprehended by us. They are spiritual, and our natural ears cannot lay hold of that which is spiritual. The spiritual must clothe itself with the material, in order that men, who dwell in the body, may take cognizance of it. The thoughts must take outward form in words. The words are not the thoughts; the thoughts are not the words; but they correspond to each other, the one being on the natural plane what the other is on the spiritual plane. Thus do we have a still further illustration of the law of Discrete Degrees.

The body lives from the presence of the spirit within it; but how does the spirit itself live? We must remember that it is no less a created object, or form of life, than the body itself. There is but one uncreated source of being, and that is the Infinite Creator; He *is* life, and imparts life to all things that exist. They have no life in and of themselves, but are receptacles of life from Him. The soul or spirit of man is such a receptacle. It is filled and fed with the influences which minister to its growth and development, as surely as the body is nourished by the food which nature supplies. We have no more power to love and think of ourselves, than we have to act of ourselves. Love and wisdom, or goodness and truth, entering into our minds, and causing the activities of affection and thought, are as much a gift of God as are the natural rain and sunshine. The soul is the life of the body, but the breath or spirit of God, received by each one according to his form and nature, is the life of the soul. To sum up briefly: Life flows from within outwards. The Lord God himself is its inmost fountain. From Him it proceeds by successive steps or degrees which constitute the different planes or levels of the spiritual world, until in the natural bodies of men and in other fixed substances of nature it has reached its outmost limits. God is the first cause, and the spiritual world, considered in a general way as one great whole, is the mediate cause, of physical being.

From all these things it follows that the spiritual world is a world of causes in its relation to the natural world, which, therefore, is a world of effects. As the life of the body is communicated to it through the spirit, the bodily condition must be more or less affected by the spiritual condition. The close relationship between the mind and the body has been frequently observed, and is, to some extent at least, recognized by physicians. It has been known that a morbid or discouraged mental state is unfavorable to recovery from sickness, whereas, if the patient can be brought into a bright and cheerful frame of mind, the prospect is deemed more hopeful. But while this general truth has been seen, there has been no full apprehension of the fact that all natural disorders of every kind have a spiritual origin. If men had lived from the beginning in the true order which was divinely appointed for them, they would not have been subject to the physical ailments under which they suffer. To a certain extent, this spiritual cause of disease is plainly manifest; as, for instance, if a man goes to excess in the indulgence of any natural appetite, he has to pay the penalty in bodily pain or weakness of some sort. The habitual drunkard grows helplessly imbecile or prematurely old; the signs of his indulgence are visible in the loss of vigor, and, not unfrequently, in the inroads of marked forms of disease. In like manner, any mental habit which violates the divine laws of being, always tends to produce abnormal bodily conditions. Who can doubt, for example, that complete self-absorption, with the propensity to dwell on one's own ailments, misfortunes, or grievances, tends to bring about unnatural states of body as well as of mind? We must remember that the spiritual world has its evil as well as its good side. It comprises hell as well as heaven; and so far as we cherish what is evil in ourselves, we come into association with hell and with the infernal spirits who are there, just as we invite the companionship of angels whenever our hearts are turned to what is good and true. Accordingly we find Swedenborg saying: —

> Diseases have correspondence with the spiritual world. They have not correspondence with heaven, but with those who are in the opposite, thus with those who are in the hells. By the spiritual world, in the universal sense, is meant both heaven and hell; for man, when he dies, passes out of the natural world into the spiritual world. That diseases have correspondence with those who are in the hells, is because diseases correspond to the lusts and passions of the mind; the latter also are the origins of diseases; for the origins of diseases in general are different forms of intemperance, likewise the various kinds of pleasures merely corporeal, also envyings, hatreds, revenges, lasciviousness, and the like, which destroy the interiors of man, and when these are destroyed the exteriors suffer, and draw man into disease and thus into death. . . . From these things it may be manifest that diseases have correspondence with the spiritual world, but with unclean things there; for diseases in themselves

are unclean, inasmuch as they originate in things unclean, as was said above. (Arcana Cœlestia, 5712.)

If these statements are true — and surely there is no reason to doubt them — it would appear that, far more frequently than men are aware, they may bring diseases upon themselves by cherishing evil thoughts and feelings, which, if they would, they might avoid. They open the door to infernal influences by allowing themselves to indulge a sinful imagination, or to brood over their fancied wrongs, or to build unprofitable castles in the air which serve to keep them from an orderly and useful life among men. All these unhealthy conditions of mind predispose a man to unhealthy conditions of body. If one is indolent, he abstains from needful exercise; if he lets his imagination dwell on the pleasures of the table, he is prone to overload his stomach with unwholesome food; if he gives the reins to any form of sensual lust, he subjects his body to a current of morbid and feverish activities whose essence is infernal. We know not how far our own pains and weaknesses may be due to evil states and feelings in the mind; but of this we may feel certain, that if there had been no sin, there would be no sickness. The world around man would not have been capable of producing sickness, if there had not first been something wrong in the world within him, which gave the original impulse.

This relation between mental and bodily disorders seems to be plainly indicated by the fact that our

Lord, when He was in the world, associated the two with each other. He said to the man sick with palsy, " Thy sins be forgiven thee ;" and His oft-repeated declaration to those whom He healed was, " Thy faith hath made thee whole," or, " According to thy faith be it unto thee." We shall presently see that we have no right to draw from these facts any sweeping conclusions with regard to what is ordinarily possible among men. But they manifestly confirm the general law of connection between the natural and the spiritual, showing that the Lord's power to heal men's bodies made one with the influence which He brought to bear on the evils that oppressed their souls. By the conflict which He was waging against infernal spirits, He gained control, such as no one else ever had, over the spiritual sources of disease, and thus restored the sick to health and strength. But this was only a secondary matter. His real and essential work was that of saving them from their sins, and of making sure for them the eternal blessedness of heaven.

Let us then endeavor to maintain healthy and normal states of mind; let us not knowingly cherish anything that is evil. This course of action will unquestionably be a safeguard against disease, for the reasons which have already been stated. A sound mind tends always to produce a sound body. But, at this point we must call a halt. We must not fall into the mistake of supposing that in the present state of the world all bodily disease and infirmity can be accounted for by reference to mental conditions existing in the patient, or can be traced to the particular sins of those who are afflicted. On the contrary, we well know that among those who suffer the pains of sickness are often included the best of men and women. Many a sick chamber is more full of the atmosphere of heaven, than any other place on earth. Moreover, even infants and young children are not exempt from bodily ailments and sufferings. Other factors, therefore, must be recognized in this matter, beside that of personal transgression. The intemperate man or the libertine not only brings disease upon himself, but may transmit the seeds of it to his posterity. The same must be true of those who indulge more subtle evils. That diseases, no less than deeper characteristics, are hereditary, is a well-attested fact. Thus they are, indeed, the effect or consequence of evil. But, being indirectly and unconsciously communicated, they are something for which the individual is not responsible, and they cannot by any means always be removed by efforts on his part to rise into a higher atmosphere of spiritual life.

Again, we must not forget that the natural world, in which we live as to our bodies, is a real world, and an essential part of the created universe. Of itself it is, indeed, dead, being animated and vivified by the spiritual world within it, as the body is animated and vivified by the soul. But within its own domain it is subject to conditions quite distinct from its relation to anything higher. It constitutes one great whole, with all its parts related to and dependent upon each other. If any part becomes disordered or disarranged, the whole is more or less sensibly affected. What, for example, would become of the earth or her sister planets, if the sun were to be extinguished and blotted out of existence? What would the animal kingdom do, if the vegetable kingdom were to be destroyed? Again, how could our bodies live, if in the world around them there were nothing to minister to their sustenance? They must not only be filled with life from a higher plane, but must receive strength and support from things on the lower plane to which they themselves belong. The earth, no less than the heavens, is the Lord's, and He hath given it to the children of men. "He hath put all things under their feet." That is to say, He has made natural or physical objects for man's service. There is not one of them but contributes to the fulness and perfection of his life while he lives on earth; and no small portion of them is absolutely essential to his earthly existence. In a word, nature has its own laws which must be kept, in order to receive the full benefit of our life here below. Those laws are entirely distinct from spiritual laws, just as nature itself is distinct from spirit. In other words, the laws are divided by Discrete Degrees from each other, yet in reality they make one. Whatever is conducive to orderly life in this world, corresponds to something which is conducive to orderly life in the spiritual world; whatever tends to make man's body strong and healthy, corresponds to that which strengthens his soul. The food of the body is the outward visible type of food for the spirit; but, as we have had occasion to observe so often in the course of this discussion, the two things are entirely distinct from each other, and must never be confounded. Natural laws, though corresponding to spiritual laws, must, nevertheless, be kept on their own plane, as if they were wholly separate and independent. It is, indeed, little that man knows about spiritual conditions; but he has been able, from the beginning of his existence on earth, to fulfil, at least within certain limits, the requirements needful for sustaining his bodily life during the brief period of its continuance.

Let us be sure that we clearly and fully apprehend this principle; for it bears very strongly on some considerations which are to follow. There are certain rules of life pertaining to the body, and to the body alone, which are as imperative as any other rules, so long as we live in the body. Those rules bear the same relation to the plane of nature, that other and corresponding rules bear to the plane of mind. Why is it necessary that we should eat or sleep? Why is it necessary that we should have a certain amount of air and exercise? Why do we need heat and light from the sun, and rain from the clouds? Simply because the life of our bodies is made dependent on the reception of such things as nature provides. They must appropriate to themselves these outmost gifts of the Lord's bounty, just as our minds or spirits should appropriate the internal and more precious treasures of love and truth. Hence follows another principle which has been already alluded to. If anything is out of order in the world around us, the body feels it. If there is a famine, the body suffers from hunger. If there is a drought, it suffers from thirst. If there is too great dampness or miasma in the atmosphere, the body is affected. Food of an unsuitable kind or in too great quantity, water tainted with impure substances, bad drainage, or any kind of filth or pollution, becomes the medium through which harm may reach our bodily senses and members. These outward natural conditions may themselves be due to perverted spiritual ones. Man's neglect, carelessness, or indifference may have been the means whereby the world around him is visibly corrupted; or, in deeper and more subtle ways, of which he is unconscious, these secondary causes of disease may have sprung into existence; but no reasonable person can deny that they do exist. Such being the case, they must be dealt with where they are. For the natural evil we must seek a natural palliative or remedy. The imperfect drainage system must be replaced by a better. Filth must be removed from the places which it contaminates. On the natural plane, as far as possible, all things must be set in order. And if we find in nature, as we unquestionably do, substances which serve to relieve pain and to drive away sickness, we should not hesitate to use them and to thank the Lord that He has provided these gifts also for our health and comfort. As an inhabitant of both worlds, man should hold himself amenable to the laws of both worlds, and should gratefully acknowledge his dependence on the helps which reach him from without, no less than on those which come from within.

Thus, there are three factors which enter into the consideration of bodily health and sickness: first, the life of the indwelling spirit; secondly, hereditary tendencies and influences; and thirdly, the natural environment, with all that it implies. The trouble in dealing with the subject has too often been that one or another of these factors has been lost sight of. Medical practitioners, as a class, have doubtless been disposed to rely too exclusively on external remedies. They have frequently treated the body as if it were an inanimate machine which could be patched and mended at pleasure without regard to its connection with any higher source of being. The importance of spiritual influences as affecting natural conditions has been more or less overlooked. The Christian physician, in the full, true sense, is one who follows in the footsteps of his Lord; and, while he ministers from the overflowing store-house of nature to the relief of the body, remembers that his work is, at best, only coöperation on the lower plane with the help which comes from above. This element in his effort to heal may not be made prominent in anything that he does or says; but it can hardly be absent from his thoughts, if he endeavors — as all men should, whatever be their profession or vocation — to act in the spirit of his Master.

On the other hand, there are those, especially in recent times, who maintain that the only cure for the body is to be obtained from mental or spiritual sources. Theorists of this kind abound, under such designating terms as Faith Cure, Mental Healing, and Christian Science. They discard all the medical experience of ages. They brush aside the laws of hygiene, and disregard all natural conditions. They eschew the effects of heredity, and claim that nothing is needed for restoring the body to health except some influence brought to bear upon the mind. Surely, if the manifest order of creation be taken account of — which comprehends all the planes or degrees of human life — the position thus described is fearfully one-sided; dangerously lacking in the knowledge of those physical facts and needs which must lie at the foundation of bodily health and treatment. Having seized upon one important truth, and having, perhaps, in some instances successfully applied it, they make the fatal mistake of supposing that it is the whole truth. And, as a consequence, many in the community are suffering from their narrowness and ignorance.

There is no method of treatment which does not claim to have effected its cures. The newspapers abound in advertisements of patent medicines, containing certificates, apparently genuine, from those who have experienced relief from their use. Wonderful stories are told of cures accomplished by visits to holy shrines, or by touching the dead bones of saints. Every school of medicine can furnish its proofs of successful service to men. Why should we doubt that there is some measure of truth in all these claims? Why, again, may we not believe that there are certain physical conditions which chiefly need, for their amendment, the help that comes from a change in the mental state, such change being effected sometimes in one way, and sometimes in another? The devout Roman Catholic may experience it when he comes in contact with such things as to him seem the most sacred. Others may feel it when, for the first time, they are made vividly aware of the reality of spiritual things, and there flows into their souls the strong assurance of higher help and support. But in the vast majority of cases, the needs will be different from these, and the work can be effectually done only in other ways. There is little danger that the time will ever come, as long as men have infirm bodies, when natural remedies will not be sought, and the aid of the educated physician will not be valued. Let us try to be just in our judgment of these matters; broad, comprehensive, and tolerant; not shutting our eyes to any obvious truth, but, at the same time, not pinning our faith to any partial system which arrogates to itself the exclusive power of healing.

For the reason that the philosophy of the New Church distinctly recognizes the spiritual source of life as an element which may affect even the bodily condition, there has been some slight tendency on the part of those who accept it, to favor the bold general assumption that mental or spiritual influence is the one infallible panacea. The only way in which this error can be dispelled with many who fall into it, is, doubtless, the hard way of experience. But those who can view the teachings of the Church as a whole will keep out of this pitfall. Moreover, if they carefully examine the theories of these new schools, they will find them sadly lacking in the principles which the New-Churchman sees to be most vital. Perhaps the most prominent among them is that which calls itself Christian Science, and which, like many delusions in the history of the world, has gathered to itself a large number of devoted adherents. A brief examination of the doctrines embodied in this system may not be out of place at the present time.

A primary and fundamental teaching is that there is no personal God. This is plainly stated at the very beginning of the "Platform of Christian Scientists," as formulated by Mrs. Eddy, the founder of the sect. "There is neither a personal Deity, a personal devil, nor a personal man." "God is principle and not person" (Vol. 2, p. 192). The ground for this belief is said to be that a person is necessarily finite and limited, and principle is not. As if our limited conception of personality as exemplified in human beings were the only true conception of it! As if there could be no such thing as an infinite person, a being of perfect love and wisdom, superior to the limitations of space and time! What, indeed, is the true idea of personality, unless it be that of one who loves and thinks? In the New Church, we are taught that the Lord is love itself and wisdom itself, and that love and wisdom are the life of the universe; but they do not exist in Him as mere abstractions; they are the essential elements of His personality. They are the things which cause Him to be the Infinite, Divine Person that He is. And man, too, is a person — created in the image, after the likeness, of God — because he is endowed with will and understanding, that is, with the power of receiving love and wisdom from God, and of using them as if they were his own. Take away the idea of personality from God, and he ceases to be an object of worship. All clearness of thought respecting Him is gone, and in His place you have nothing left but a vague, cold Pantheism.

Secondly, according to the creed of Christian Scientists, "Matter or the mortal body, is nothing but a belief and an illusion. When belief changes — as in dreams — matter or the mortal body, changes with it, and is wherever or whatever belief makes it" (Vol. 2, pp. 193, 194). On this assumption, the whole theory and practice of Christian Scientists rest. The body being nothing but "a belief and an illusion," its pain and sickness are a belief and an illusion also. The one thing for the patient to do is to accept this doctrine as true, and by accepting it to rise above the sense of physical suffering. Or, in other words, since there is no reality to such suffering, it becomes to him the nonentity that it is, if he can only think so. Thus the whole work of healing is made to depend on a certain act of faith in the mind. Or, to quote again from Mrs. Eddy: "Sickness is a belief, and to understand this, destroys the belief and breaks the spell of disease. To the metaphysician [which is a name applied by the Christian Scientists to themselves] sickness is a dream from which the patient needs to be awakened, which should not appear real to him, and when he makes it unreal to his patient, he cures him." (Science and Health, Vol. 1, p. 188.)

In other words, as has been shown, disease is to be driven away by the simple exercise of thought, by a confident affirmation of the mind that it is non-existent. No matter what the nature of the sickness is, it cannot withstand this mental conviction. Consider yourself well and incapable of being otherwise, and you will be well. The final test of this doctrine, as in all other cases, will be that of experience. It is sufficient for our present purpose to state that experience shows it to be repeatedly unsuccessful. Where it has failed, the blame has been conveniently laid upon lack of faith in the patient or in those by whom he was attended. Nevertheless, the fact remains that, for some reason or other, it has often, if not generally, failed. But the particular point to which I would direct attention is that the operation of this pretended law of healing is ascribed to a purely intellectual effort. One belief is cast out by another. The belief that man is sick is cast out by the belief that he is not. How different is this from the great fundamental teachings of the Scriptures, which are summed up in the saying: "If thou wouldst enter into life, keep the Commandments." If there is any fact well attested in our experience, it is that the evils of our spiritual nature cannot be removed by any mere change in our mode of thinking. Their presence with us and power over us are something which will not be thrown off by trying to ignore them. Each individual evil to which we are inclined must be shunned as sin against God; shunned, not once or twice merely, but repeatedly, as often as it makes its appearance, which it will do many, many times. And are we to suppose that our bodily ills are less stubborn, or can always be removed in a shorter and easier way? If there is any analogy between the evils which infest the mind and the disorders which affect the body, then must there be some analogy between the ways in which the two kinds of evil are got rid of. The faith of which our Lord speaks, and whose excellence He so strongly emphasizes, is not the mere faith of intellectual belief, but that which leads men to learn His will in order that they may do it. Such was the faith of those whom He made whole. They had not simply come into a changed state of mind with regard to certain matters; they were not merely inspired by a sudden confidence that He could help and save them; but their hearts and wills were touched with a deep sense of their unworthiness, and of their need of strength higher than their own, together with a sincere desire to live a life according to His teachings. Christian Science seems to be among theories relating to bodily health, what the old doctrine of salvation by faith alone was, among the so-called tenets of Christianity.

And how absurd and unreasonable the whole thing is in its denial of natural realities. These people say, "There is no such thing as matter; matter is nothing but a belief and an illusion;" and yet they go on calmly eating their three meals a day. Thrice in every twenty-four hours, they take to themselves what they pronounce "a belief and an illusion," with all the zest that is common to humanity; and they well know that if they refrained from so doing they would soon cease to live in this world. This food goes to the support of their natural bodies, which, again, they declare to be "nothing but a belief and an illusion." There is no difference between them and others in their dependence on all the gifts of nature. In summer they are warm, in winter they are cold ; and when night comes they are weary, and must rest. These mere "illusions" which we call our bodies must indeed seem to them rather hard to dispel — rather stubborn and persistent. It is difficult to treat the matter seriously, difficult to believe that the advocates of the theory are in earnest about it ; and yet the evidence is quite too positive to be called in question, that many of them are sincere, and wholly unable to perceive the inconsistencies and absurdities of their doctrine. Having been, perhaps, physically helped, as they suppose, by the mode of treatment involved in the system, and having thus been led to believe in some spiritual power, and in an influence of the mind over the body, they hasten to conclude that all its teachings are true, and embrace it as a new revelation and a new religion.

It is not unjust, in considering a system of this kind, which claims to be based on universal laws of life and to embody infallible methods of restoring physical health, to point out a palpable false statement in which gross ignorance is joined with astonishing assurance and presumption. In No. 16 of the "Platform of Christian Scientists" we read as follows : "The word Adam signifies original sin — error, and not man. Adam is from the Latin *demens*, meaning madness, to undo, to spoil" (Science and Health, Vol. 2, p. 196). The absurdity of this statement will be at once apparent to one who has the least knowledge of the history of language. "Adam" is a Hebrew word occurring hundreds of times in the Old Testament, and rightly translated by its English equivalent "man." To say that this word, which is so common in the oldest book in the world, was derived from a word in the Latin language, which was not known until centuries after the Bible had been written, is to make an assertion that is indeed ridiculous, and may well throw doubts over the writer's claims even to common honesty and intelligence.

But, not to dwell on these secondary matters, in what sharp contrast does the doctrine that there is no personal God and that all nature is but a fantastic illusion, stand with the teachings familiar to New-Churchmen; namely, that God is truly our Father, revealed to us in the Divinely human form and nature of our Lord Jesus Christ; that He is the source of our life, the Giver of our blessings and the true object of our worship; that according as we keep His laws and shun evils as sins against Him, we are enabled, in our finite degree, to become like Him; that He has created us to be both internal and external, both spiritual and natural; that His mercy surrounds us on all sides, that it meets us in the rays of the sun, in the food we eat, in the air we breathe, and in all earthly blessings, as well as in the deeper and more vital influences which sustain the life of our souls — that all these things, being His gifts, are real; not, indeed, having life of themselves, but being filled with life from Him, just as the body of itself is dead, but lives from the spirit which is within it! Thus, and thus only, can we see and believe that all things which God has created for the use and enjoyment of man are very good. Thus only can we respond to the exclamation of the Psalmist, "O Lord, our Lord, how excellent is Thy name *in all the earth.*"

There is another class of believers in spiritual influences as being the sole and sufficient means of promoting bodily health, of whom we should speak with respect and gentleness, though we cannot accept their opinions. They are those who so interpret the Gospels as to think that the power which the Lord gave His immediate disciples over disease, was equally given to all who at any future time might pay Him their allegiance. "These signs," so it is said in the last chapter of the Gospel according to Mark, "shall follow them that believe: In my name shall they cast out devils; they shall speak with new tongues; they shall take up serpents; and if they drink any deadly thing, it shall not hurt them; they shall lay hands on the sick, and they shall recover." There was, as we know, a literal fulfilment of these promises in the days immediately succeeding the Lord's resurrection and ascension. We read in the book of Acts, how the Apostles did cast out devils, speak with new tongues, take up serpents without harm, and heal the sick by the laying on of hands. But the fact that they were able to do these things, by no means proves that the ability to do them would be perpetual. The time in which they lived was an exceptional one. It was a crisis in the affairs of men and in the history of the world. An unusual state of things existed which called for unusual treatment. Ordinary proofs of the Lord's divine nature and authority would not have sufficed in that dark and unbelieving age; so that evidences which we call miracles, because they are contrary to our ordinary experience, were necessary for convincing men of His authority, and for establishing His kingdom. After these events had taken place, and had been duly recorded in the Gospel narratives and in the Apostolic writings, the knowledge of them as thus written was sufficient to carry similar conviction to succeeding generations; and the exceptional conditions of that particular period ceased to exist. On this subject Swedenborg writes as follows : —

The Jewish nation only believed in Jehovah on account of His miracles; for they were external men, and these are impelled to Divine worship only by external things, such as miracles, which strike their minds. A miraculous faith was also the first faith with those with whom the new [Christian] Church was to be established; and it is also first with all in the Christian world at this day, wherever the miracles performed by the Lord are preached. For the first faith with all is an historical faith, which afterwards becomes saving when man by his life becomes spiritual. (Apocalypse Explained, 815.)

That is to say, in the beginning of the Christian Church, ocular evidence of the Lord's power over all things disorderly and evil was essential as a means of leading men to believe in Him. The kind of faith thus produced, however, was not genuine faith of the heart; but prepared the way for it, and afterwards ceased to be necessary. So, too, a knowledge of the fact that the Lord performed such miracles when He was in the world, and that His disciples performed them by virtue of His presence with them, serves a similar purpose for those who may read about it in the New Testament and are thereby led to perceive that He was no mere man like themselves. But, after a while, if they continue to grow in Christian faith and life, they are no longer influenced by a mere belief in the verity of certain historical events. On the contrary, their faith becomes a living trust in a divinely human Lord, who has all power in heaven and on earth, who is always present with them to help and to save, and who by His providence, seeks ever to lead them in such ways as will most surely promote their everlasting welfare. As they read the Gospel story in this spirit, and with the recognition of this deeper truth respecting Him, they see that bodily healing was but a mere incident — but one of the ways whereby He gave expression to the higher work which He was doing, namely, that of overcoming the enemies of men's souls; and they know that, whether they be afflicted with physical diseases or not, they have in themselves evil tendencies which correspond to leprosy, palsy, fevers, and all other forms of sickness that the Lord healed; and they know, furthermore, that He is continually endeavoring, so far as they will permit Him, to remove these evils from them in order that his unchanging purpose of bringing them into heaven, may be fulfilled. The abnormal conditions, peculiar to a time like that of which the Gospels treat, have passed away, and there is no more need of a day of Pentecost when cloven tongues of fire shall appear, and the disciples shall speak in many languages; there is no reason why the viper's deadly poison should cease to produce its usual effects, or the ordinary laws of nature, which are also the laws of God, should be apparently suspended. For a faith has been, or should have been, implanted in their hearts, which does not depend on such things as these, and which binds them to their Lord and Master with the cords of a deeper, truer, and holier relationship.

These considerations naturally lead us to reflect on the ways of the Lord's providence, among which, if we think truly, we cannot fail to recognize the fact that by means of lesser evils He often seeks to ward off or prevent greater ones. The absolute freedom of men is essential to their spiritual growth and progress. The Divine interpositions which we call miracles are not common, because they would have the effect of destroying this freedom. But the fact that man is free carries with it the possibility of his doing evil rather than good, although he knows that the evil is forbidden. So far as evil exists in the world, it causes unhappy consequences; it tends to produce disorder of all kinds, spiritual, moral, natural, physical. Now, as we well know, or should know, these evils are, under the wonderful providence of God, made serviceable for their own correction. If a man experiences in his own body the effect of wrong-doing, he is thereby warned to abstain from it ever after. And if the Lord sees that by means of physical suffering our characters can be built up and strengthened, and our spiritual life throughout eternity may be made more useful and happy, He permits it to come upon us. This outward evil does not proceed from Him any more than other evils do; for He is love or goodness itself, and is no more capable of evil than the sun is capable of emitting rays of dense blackness. All evil is, as has been previously said or implied, the direct or indirect effect of man's misuse of his freedom; but the Lord, watching over him with infinite love and wisdom, permits these lower effects to manifest themselves in such ways that they may most surely react upon the hidden causes from which they spring. This is indeed a profound subject, and we can only touch, as it were, upon its borders; but, surely, our experience must have been narrow and our observation superficial, unless we have learned from all the lessons of life, that what we call misfortunes, whether they take the form of disappointed ambition, loss of property, or bodily sickness, are often, yea, always, blessings in disguise, through which higher and nobler possibilities are opened before us, through the infinite mercy of Him who knows our needs far better than we ourselves can know them.

The law that lesser evils may assist in the removal of greater ones, has its application even on the plane of man's physical being. It explains why drugs, even those which are poisonous, may be efficacious in curing bodily disease. "Things harmful to man," says Swedenborg, "are serviceable in absorbing malignities, and thus as remedies" (Divine Love and Wisdom, no. 336). In other words, substances taken into the body, which in too great quantities or under other conditions might be hurtful, attract to themselves, in a state of disease, the malignant germs or humors which, from a merely external point of view, are the essence of the disease, and, passing out of the body, carry the disease with them. Thus Divine providence concurs with the remedies which man applies, and bodily sickness is relieved. Here, again, a large field of inquiry is opened, which we can only touch upon in the briefest possible way; but this brief allusion may serve to suggest a reason why the reception into the system of things essentially harmful, may yet be a method whereby the Lord works for the restoration of order and health in the lowest, as in every other degree of man's life. The evils which are overruled for good, are no less under the Divine care and tributary to the Divine purposes, than agencies, intrinsically excellent, which minister directly to the creation and preservation of the universe.

The great truth, however, which comprehends all other truths, is that "the Lord God Omnipotent reigneth." In His hands are the issues of life and death. "He hath made us, and not we ourselves." He has caused us for a while to live in this natural world, clothed with natural bodies; but the true purpose of our existence is spiritual and eternal. In His sight, our life here on earth is wholly subsidiary to the never-ending life hereafter. His providence has primary regard to our preparation for that life, to the end that it may be a happy one, in which all our faculties shall be brought into the freest exercise and trained for everlasting usefulness. Sooner or later, death will set its seal upon our earthly bodies, and we shall wake to consciousness in that inner spiritual world, which, from the first moment of our creation, has been our home. Then shall we see clearly the meaning of all our experiences. Then shall we understand the uses of the trials through which we have passed. Then shall we know that it was not possible for the kind and wise providence which presided over our lives, to let us suffer a single moment's pain that could not be made serviceable in the development of our spiritual character. Still further, we shall see that all the springs of our being are in Him. From Him come all our life and strength and health. Now, as ever, He is the good Physician. Through whatever channel relief comes when we are in distress of body or mind, it proceeds from Him. He meets us in the inmost chambers of our souls. He fills our hearts with good and our minds with truth, and provides for us all the healthful influences of nature. "He forgiveth all our iniquities; He healeth all our diseases; He redeemeth our life from destruction, and crowneth us with loving-kindness and tender mercies." So far as it is good for men to be spared the discipline of sickness, He will either withhold it from them or will provide the means of cure. We can fear no danger if we really believe that underneath are His everlasting arms. And while we should not relax our efforts to make the conditions of this life comfortable, and to maintain sound bodies as the dwelling places of sound minds, our first and chief endeavor should be to work with Him for the establishment of that permanent happy state after the labors of this world are ended, when "there shall be no more death, neither sorrow nor crying; for the former things are passed away."

www.ingramcontent.com/pod-product-compliance
Lightning Source LLC
Chambersburg PA
CBHW032224230426
43666CB00033B/1206